My First
NEW YORK

My First
NEW YORK

EARLY ADVENTURES
IN THE BIG CITY

{ AS REMEMBERED BY ACTORS, ARTISTS,
ATHLETES, CHEFS, COMEDIANS, FILMMAKERS,
MAYORS, MODELS, MOGULS, PORN STARS,
ROCKERS, WRITERS, AND OTHERS }

EDITED BY
DAVID HASKELL
AND ADAM MOSS

ecco
An Imprint of HarperCollinsPublishers

Portions of this book appeared previously in *New York* magazine and on nymag.com.

HarperCollins books may be purchased for educational, business, or sales promotional use. For information please write: Special Markets Department, HarperCollins Publishers, 10 East 53rd Street, New York, NY 10022.

A hardcover edition of this book was published in 2010 by Ecco, an imprint of HarperCollins Publishers.

FIRST ECCO PAPERBACK EDITION PUBLISHED 2012.

Designed by Suet Yee Chong

Library of Congress Cataloging-in-Publication Data has been applied for.

ISBN 978-0-06-196394-0

12 13 14 15 16   OV/RRD   10 9 8 7 6 5 4 3 2 1

I came into New York an emperor on a barge. It wasn't the skipper who was taking the boat in, but my will to conquer, and I was almost sorry for the New York that would have to yield so completely to my demands.

—SINCLAIR LEWIS,
"THAT WAS NEW YORK—AND THAT WAS ME" (1903)

I'm going to New York!
(what a lark! what a song!)

—FRANK O'HARA,
"SONG" (1951)

Contents

Preface

This book started out as a magazine feature that, like the city it celebrated, soon grew a bit crowded for its size. In April of 2009, *New York* magazine published a cover story in which thirty local notables recounted their first New York experience. These true tales—comic, clueless, heartwarming, and unusually candid—had struck a chord in the office as they were filed. But the response they received upon publication, and the outpouring of readers' own stories at nymag.com, made us realize we were onto something deeper than a collection of newbie anecdotes, however memorable: that one's arrival in this city was a memory as primal, potent, and private (yet begging to be shared) as that other First Time. So we decided to widen the net. The result, *My First New York*, expands some of the stories that ran in the magazine, and adds many, many more New Yorkers willing to tell their tale.

For this book, a few of the writers wrote, the rest—a mix of actors, artists, comedians, entrepreneurs, filmmakers, journalists, musicians, politicians, sports stars, and others—talked. For all of them, recounting their first adventures in New York seemed to bring out their truest selves: Liz Smith gossiped while Liza Minnelli gushed; Yogi Berra kept it very, very simple. And they went about moving in very different ways: some, like actress Lauren Hutton, came on a glorious impulse; some (or at least blog magnate Nick Denton) made a detailed spreadsheet that assigned weighted scores to various cities, and then fiddled with the calculations until New York came up the winner. Few have arrived with less than filmmaker Jonas Mekas, a concentration-camp survivor on a UN refugee ship; few have swanned in with more than Diane von Furstenberg, a *princess.* An extraordinary number managed to land in New York just as something historic was happening—but then again, something historic happens here a lot. Cindy Sherman arrived in the middle of the Summer of Sam; Danny Meyer came on the day John Lennon was shot.

Arranged chronologically, their stories combine into a subjective and impressionistic history of our city, one that captures its changing temper and tone since the Great Depression. Through the arrivals' wide eyes, we watch New York's transformation from the land of jazz clubs and the World's Fair to a seething pit where college faculty revolted alongside students and empty lofts awaited colonization, to the kind of place where dot-com millionaires took cooking lessons and you needed serious connections to snag a job at a video store. They tell of a city that seesawed from safe to dangerous and back—and then dangerous again, but in a different way. And together they make an accidental encyclopedia of New York hot spots through the ages, because that's where the newcomers in search of their crowd inevitably gravitate: from the Cedar Tavern and the Gaslight to Lutèce and Elaine's, from Max's Kansas City and the Mudd Club to the Odeon and Bungalow 8, they're all here, dots on the unbroken line of the Next Next Things.

A recent survey found that more than half of all New Yorkers have moved here from somewhere else. And, in fact, the city is a magnet that attracts in times good and bad. Roughly the same number of foreign immigrants (about 750,000) moved to New York during the 1970s downturn as during the boom years that just ended. It is also a bit of a sieve: even as the city serves as a mere gateway to America to millions of immigrants, there is always the subset who look up and realize that moving any farther would be redundant at best. They are joined by about eighty thousand Americans who arrive each year from elsewhere in the country. As it is often said, what makes one a real New Yorker is the conscious decision to become one.

"It's one thing to become a New Yorker," notes Keith Hernandez, who was traded to the Mets midseason in 1983. "It's so much weirder to become a New Yorker that all the other New Yorkers know." It is true that an inordinate percentage of people in this book are in the second camp: they have won the lottery, conquered the city in one way or another. For some, the red carpet was laid out at once (Naomi Campbell's account begins with the words "At sixteen years old, I was summoned by Anna Wintour"). For others, it unspooled through roach-infested illegal sublets and late night commutes back to Jersey.

There is one chronicler here who you certainly will not have heard of—yet. As part of the feature that ran in the magazine, we put a call out to readers to find the city's most recent arrivals. We heard from hundreds of brand-new New Yorkers, and chose one—Jenny Joslin—to complete the collection. She's twenty-three years old, hails from Texas, and aspires to be an actress. The direction of Joslin's career remains to be seen, but like the others in the book, success is, weirdly enough, beside the point. What you are holding is a collection of fifty-six testaments to a larger revelation, one that arrivals of all stripes and all eras have experienced again and again, regardless of how the city proceeds to treat them. It is something songwriter Rufus Wainwright terms "having cracked the code of living life to the fullest." Becoming a New Yorker is a bit of a victory in itself, and so every story in this book has a happy ending by default. It comes with the territory.

DAVID DINKINS

{ former mayor
arrived: 1933 }

I was born and raised during my early years in Trenton, New Jersey. But when my parents separated, when I was six, I moved to Harlem with my mother. Governor Roosevelt had just become President Roosevelt. We had the Great Depression, of course, but the Harlem Renaissance still had some life in it. Seventh Avenue was a boulevard in those days, and every Easter, everyone would march up and down it in their finery. I remember when Joe Louis was winning fights and people would open their windows and share the radios they had. I didn't see more joy and pride until, well, until those same streets and fire escapes were filled with cheers on election night 2008.

We moved a lot. The joke was that we moved when the rent was due. My mother and grandmother both worked as domestics, each making a dollar a day. But I made some money, too. I'd go to 125th and Eighth, where all the pushcarts were selling groceries. I bought shopping bags, three for a nickel, and I sold them at two cents apiece. I would save up and buy my mother something nice from the five-and-dime store.

I wasn't always such a good little boy. I had a skater scooter—a soapbox and a two-by-four with roller skates on the bottom. Most kids decorated their skater scooters with bottle caps from soda bottles. But if you were really cool you had reflectors. Thing was, you couldn't just buy a reflector; you had to liberate them from cars. So I was out there liberating with my friends, and a police officer caught me because I was the littlest in the group. And he brought me home and told my mother and grandmother that their good little boy had done this. It was a total shock to them. Now, heretofore, all they had to do was give me a look of disappointment, and I'd be crying in thirty seconds. But now we were living in this city, and things were changing. They stripped me bare, stood me up in the bathtub, and hit me good with some leather straps. I never did anything bad again.

LORIN MAAZEL

I was born in Paris and grew up on the West Coast, but at nine years old, I came to conduct an orchestra for the New York World's Fair. It made a mark. The *New York Times* picked up the story, and when Mayor La Guardia heard that there was a child conducting an orchestra, he called me into his office in one of the pavilions. We had a conversation, and there's a little picture in the archives of me, my finger up, expounding on something, telling the mayor how to run the city.

Years later, when our family had moved to Pittsburgh, I would come to New York. I would perform a Friday-evening concert in Pittsburgh, and then I would drive that night to the Big Apple in a DeSoto that I had picked up in some used-car lot. I'd have all day in the city on Saturday, and then I'd get up at five in the morning to drive back in time for the three o'clock Sunday concert. I went to nightclubs, museums, Central Park. If I had a girlfriend, I'd take her to the movies. We never had any money, even for gasoline, so sometimes my buddy and I would take our fiddles to a nightclub where they would give us a meal or a little bit of money if we played tunes for the customers. We'd play Cole Porter and George Gershwin, and also a bit of Mozart or Bartók—pieces written for two violins. If we got too classical, however, the proprietor would come by and start frowning at us until we broke into some well-known tune of the day.

YOGI
BERRA

{ baseball player
arrived: 1946 }

New York? It was big.

CHITA
RIVERA

} actress and singer {
arrived: 1948

One day George Balanchine sent a scout from the School of American Ballet to the Jones-Haywood School in Washington, D.C., where I was a fifteen-year-old studying dance. We didn't know we were auditioning, or who George Balanchine was. But I was picked and sent to New York to perform for him. I remember my foot got a blister, and he stopped my audition and sent for a Band-Aid and a pair of scissors. He put my foot in his lap. If I had realized who he was, I would have dropped dead. But everyone just watched as he cut the thing away, put a Band-Aid on my blister, and we continued.

I guess I was excited to be chosen for a scholarship, but mostly I was surprised that my mother allowed me to go to New York. I was fifteen! Especially in those days, nobody let their child out of their sight. But she was brave and let me move in with my father's brother's family in the Bronx.

I went to Taft High School near the Grand Concourse and the ballet school in Midtown, so all I knew was Fifty-ninth Street and Madison Avenue, the subway, and the Bronx. I do remember looking up one day on the subway and seeing a man expose himself. That was a hell of an experience! I learned never to look up on the subway again.

At home we never went out to restaurants—who had the money?—but at the ground floor of the ballet school there was a Horn & Hardart, which was the first kind of fast food. They'd have glasses with lemon available for anyone who wanted to buy iced tea. Us dancers would come down, fill the glasses with water, and sit down and drink "lemonade" we didn't pay for.

At nineteen I got my first job in *Call Me Madam*. By then I knew that ballet wasn't for me. The world of theater was different—more relaxed, not as frightening, more like a variety show. Broadway had great shows at the time—*The King and I, Guys and Dolls*— and the streets were full of stagehands and dancers. That was what helped me get to love New York and made me feel like I owed it something.

Every other night all of us gypsies would go to Sid and Al's on West Forty-sixth and Eighth Avenue, which was run by a very sweet couple who were known to help us out if anyone needed money for food or rent. We went to hang out and share stories and attempt to feel grown up. It was my first introduction to a bar—I probably drank gin and tonics because I hadn't yet learned to order Stingers. There was always a piano there, and dancers—you know, we will dance anywhere. One night I even danced on the bar—alone. It had taken me a while to summon the courage to do something like that, but everyone else started clapping and yelling. I don't remember what song I danced to or how I danced, just that I was good.

JONAS MEKAS

{ filmmaker
arrived: 1949 }

The ocean was very stormy. We had been on the boat, my brother Adolfas and I, for seven or eight days. It was crowded, almost two thousand of us on a United Nations refugee ship. When we finally pulled up to the pier at Twenty-third Street, it was evening, and all the lights in the city were blazing. So beautiful.

Adolfas and I had papers, and our papers said that

we were supposed to go to Chicago and work in a bakery. But we looked around and thought, We're in New York City! It would be stupid to go to Chicago. So we went to Brooklyn, to live in Williamsburg with some friends who had come before us.

We were born in the Lithuanian village of Semeniškiai, where we had lived first under the Soviets, then the Germans. We had been sent to a Nazi labor camp in Elmshorn, then had escaped, hiding for two months on a farm near the Danish border. From there we were moved to the displacement camps in Wiesbaden and Kassel, and then finally the refugee boat. It was all just misery and displacement and suffering and loss. Now, suddenly, everything was bright and exciting and available. The streets of New York were open markets, like something out of Cairo. We bought three or four oranges on our first day. Here we are! We can buy fruit! It was like a miracle. Even simply to eat a real egg, and not the powdered eggs of the camps.

Williamsburg in that time was a very poor immigrant community, with many saloons and Lithuanians. (This was when people in Williamsburg were truly poor and not just doing a pretend performance of poverty.) People mostly wanted to survive—to have a job and to live like everyone else. But I did not want to live like everyone else. On the second day, Adolfas and I woke up and looked at the *New York Times* and found two well-known films—*The Cabinet of Dr. Caligari* and *The Fall of the House of Usher*—playing at a theater on Twenty-ninth Street between Sixth Avenue and Seventh Avenue. We became gluttons, absorbing everything: concerts, films, readings, conversations. I was especially interested in books. In the displacement camps, I would sell cigarettes for books. And I remember walking on Fourth Avenue south of Fourteenth Street, near where the Strand is now, and seeing nothing but bookstores. I remember the smell of it.

I was never choosy about jobs—I would take anything. One of my first was cleaning old parts of ship machinery, a very oily and dirty job. I remember very clearly working at a bed factory in Queens, where work would end at five o'clock and I would have only thirty minutes to rush to the 5:30 screenings at MoMA. People would look at this shabby, smelly person in his displacement jacket, but nobody ever bothered me. Maybe the only job that I would not take is a policeman, because in those days in New York it was fashionable to yell at police officers, "Stop being such a Nazi pig!" I would think, What do you know of Nazis?

I was very lucky to move to this city at that time. My friends Tennessee Williams, Arthur Miller, Robert Frank, Allen Ginsberg, Andy Warhol, Diane Arbus: we were all starting. We were all new. It was very special, after so many years in Europe that seemed only to be about the ends of things, to be in a time of beginnings. We would drink and eat at the Cedar Tavern or the White Horse Tavern. And when all the places in the Village would close at night, there was a twenty-four-hour night cafeteria for the taxi drivers at Twenty-ninth Street and Park Avenue South.

Two weeks after I arrived, I borrowed $300 to buy a Bolex 16mm camera. I took photos of everything, and made a fifteen-minute film about my thoughts upon arriving here. New York really saved my sanity. I had come here so despondent with civilization, and the city got me to believe in passion again. The Metropolitan Opera House was at Thirty-ninth Street and Broadway. When they destroyed that theater, I had spent so much time there that I had to take a piece of it. I still have it. It's a chunk of hard plaster from the interior decoration. People think, Oh, he is experimental and avant-garde, always looking for the new things. Not always. This city makes even the experimenters sentimental.

LIZ SMITH

{ gossip columnist
arrived: 1949 }

New York had gone dark for the war—they had thought it was going to be bombed—but by the time I arrived everybody was relieved and the city was electric with things. *South Pacific* and *Kiss Me, Kate* were opening. The theater was just booming. Of course, everything was new to me.

I had just gotten out of the University of Texas,

having gone back to school after getting married and divorced. I arrived on a train, and at Penn Station a wandering vagrant tried to get into the phone booth with me. I was pretty staggered and thought, what the hell? What a great beginning is this?

It was absolutely idiotic that Scotty, my friend from Texas, and her boyfriend, Floyd, were not there to meet me. Instead, I made my way to the hotel, and I remember noticing how dark and unwelcoming the streets were and wondering if I had made a mistake. The next night, though, Floyd brought his car in from Jersey, and we all drove up into Times Square. That was one of the most thrilling things that had ever happened to me.

I had been a terrible wife and the first in my family to get a divorce, but I arrived in New York and nobody even noticed. Scotty and I rented an apartment on Eighty-first and Central Park West. We realized immediately that we couldn't afford it, so we looked in the newspapers for a roommate. We didn't like the one we found—she was just some nebbishy kid, I don't remember her name, poor thing—and three months later we were making enough money to throw her out.

I went to work as a typist for the National Orchestra

Association. I only had about $50, but you could ride the subway for a dime and buy a ticket for a Broadway show for $2.50. I saw Carol Channing in *Gentlemen Prefer Blondes* one of the first months I was here. Still, I was bent on survival and went everywhere applying for better jobs. I showed them what a fabulous writer I was and what I'd done at the University of Texas, and they couldn't care less. I couldn't even get arrested.

Three months into this insane effort I saw in an item that Zachary Scott, a Hollywood actor from Texas whom I'd profiled in my college paper, was in New York. I found him in the phone book, and he said, "Liz! How great that you're here." He said to go to *Modern Screen* magazine at 11:00 am and tell the editor he sent me. That guy hired me cold.

Floyd, Scotty, and I would go out to bars in the Village. One night we were at a place called Seven Oaks, and a very nice man came over and bought us drinks. Scotty and I went to the ladies room and she said, "You know, Liz-O, I think that guy is as queer as a $5 bill." And I said, "Scotty, $5 is not queer." But then I realized she was right: we were in a gay bar and didn't know it!

Gay men in those days wore suits and little narrow ties—they were very elegant. When my brother, Bobby, came to the city, he worked as a waiter at a gay restaurant, which he liked a lot. He was beautiful, like a movie star, and he enjoyed having to fend them off every night. I was more narrow-minded. I had never seen any gay people before, and it was fascinating.

The most dreary thing in New York was to go to a female gay bar. They were just awful. But they were safe, since they were run by the Mafia and the Mafia was very rigid about good behavior. A guy I knew used to take me there because he thought it was funny.

I couldn't stand having a hangover, but Bobby didn't know what one was. We lived for a time in one big room with two beds. We didn't have any money, so we'd go to the Automat and eat crackers and catsup. I remember walking around the city with $3 in my pocket and lucking into things—going into bars and nursing a drink and seeing some great nightclub act perform. That was one of the happiest times of my life, before I knew Bobby was an alcoholic.

After Scotty and Floyd got married and moved on, my roommate was a wonderful Jewish girl named Shirley Herz. I hate to say that all my friends were Jewish, but they were. I absorbed all their culture, and by the end of the year I spoke a little Yiddish. When my father came to visit me, his racism just astonished me. We went to the Women's Exchange, a very elegant, Episcopalian place where women brought their embroidery, and he said, "This looks like the first civilized place with white people that we've seen in New York." I was outraged. He thought I was a Communist. I didn't even know what a Communist was.

I was a kid through my first marriage and college, and I was a kid when I first got here. I wore bobby sox and little filmy blouses you could see the brassiere through. I was much like *Mad Men*'s Peggy Olson, who I think is so awful. (I dislike remembering how callow and stupid I was.) But once Mike Wallace hired me at CBS radio, I just grew up. I began to have enormous respect for hard work, and I made a study of famous, important people. I learned how to dress, how to act, how to eat properly. I had my first artichoke in New York.

About twelve years after I arrived, my mother and father came to visit again. I had killed myself taking them around to theaters and restaurants, but they couldn't wait to get back home. They had no concept of my real life, and couldn't imagine anybody wanting to live in a small apartment and go to work every day. Then one night I took them to the Metropolitan Opera to see Leontyne Price in *Aida*. My parents were blown away. Even my father thought it was great; he didn't object to a black woman playing an Egyptian. I remember that night well because it was so glamorous, and it was the only thing I ever did that impressed them.

PAUL TAYLOR

{ dancer and choreographer
arrived: 1952 }

I came to Juilliard very eager to be a dancer. I'm natu-
rally shy, but I was not intimidated. I took a chore-
ography course with Louis Horst, and studied with
Martha Graham, who later invited me to perform in
her company. She was always very grand in public, and
she would sometimes say things in class that would

shock the girls. She thought being a virgin wasn't that great.

I was terrific looking! Though I didn't really know it at the time. My body was changing from a swimmer's body—loose and long muscles—to a dancer's body. I got thicker soles on my feet. I had a lot of encouragement at Juilliard, and got the sense that I was the Next Great One. Or at least, that's what I intended to be. I didn't know if it would happen, but I felt I was ordained.

But after I left Juilliard, then it got rough. Living was hard. I found a crummy place in Hell's Kitchen— it was really smelly, and for heat in the winter you just turned on the gas oven and opened the door. I went hungry a lot, but there were Automats and Chock Full o'Nuts, and you could get a sandwich and coffee for about twenty cents. The arts community in New York was much smaller then, and we all knew each other. Painters, writers, composers—we'd all get together quite often in somebody's old loft, or the Cedar Tavern down in the Village, to talk and trade ideas. Bob Rauschenberg and Jasper Johns both designed costumes and set pieces for me. I helped them do window displays at Tiffany, and would listen as they talked about being anti–Abstract Expressionism and wanting to change the whole scene. One night at the Cedar Tavern Jackson Pollock was very drunk, and he started shouting "I am nature!" I remember thinking that was great and true.

JAMES ROSENQUIST

{ artist
arrived: 1955 }

I hadn't yet turned twenty-one. I got notice that I had received a scholarship to the Art Students League of New York, so I took the red-eye Lockheed Electra propeller plane from Minneapolis. I had called the Sloane House YMCA on Thirty-fourth Street, and they said that if you make your own bed it's $1.79 a night. I checked in, then walked up to the ASL on

Fifty-seventh Street, and there was the secretary—her name was Rosina Florio, she later became the executive director—and I jumped on her desk and said, "Hooray! I made it. I'm in New York now!" She got a hell of a kick out of that.

I left the YMCA when I heard that someone had gotten killed there two nights before. I went first to a rooming house on West Fifty-seventh Street ($8.50 a week), and then to another one on Columbus Circle run by an old lady who had a dog standing on the bed in every room. I took the one with the smallest dog.

I was a lower-middle-class kid from Minnesota who knew what every car looked like. Then I got to New York and I never stepped in a car. I never took the subway either, and didn't have money for a cab, so I walked and wore out my feet. Existence was so inexpensive. You could go to the Metropolitan Museum for free, and the Staten Island Ferry was a nickel for an ocean voyage.

After a year, a friend from ASL told me about a job working for the Stearns family (of Bear Stearns fame) at their mansion in Irvington, twenty-five miles north of the city. The job was being a chauffeur, bartender, and occasional babysitter. I lived on the top floor, and all I really had to do was wear a button-down shirt and Bermuda shorts. I spent a year with them, living a high lifestyle. They'd throw many parties, where I'd meet people like George Reeves, Romare Bearden, and John Chamberlain, who I became friends with. Roland Stearns was Jewish, but he'd say things like, "Good morning, old sport." He inherited $16 million on his thirtieth birthday, and for the party I carved his head on a big chunk of ice.

I knew that wasn't my place, so I drove back to New York in their 1956 Lincoln convertible. I decided to find work painting billboard pictures. I had already been in the painters' union in Minneapolis, so I walked into the International Sign, Pictorial, and Display Union Local 230 on Twenty-eighth Street and requested to transfer. It took a while, but finally I got a job painting a Hebrew National salami sign on the Flatbush Extension.

I had painted pictures in Minneapolis, but I didn't know how to do lettering. I was fired in a month, at which point I started practicing on rooftops. My next job was with an ad firm in Brooklyn, which sent me to Stauch's Bath in Coney Island. I worked with my assistant Red from Red Hook twenty feet above these big fat ladies who came out naked to get a suntan. "Red," I said, "we better say something or we'll be arrested for being peeping Toms." So I shouted, "Good morning, goyls!" One woman said to her friend, "Don't worry Sadie, they don't look anyway." And then Red threw his cig down on the tarp and it caught fire and the ladies ran off the roof, screaming and naked.

I didn't have any hobbies except artwork. I was just striving to do something, because I knew I had some talent and I was pretty good and I was still trying to get better. I did meet a southern girl named Peggy Smith, a party reporter who'd invite me to all sorts of social things. She'd say, "Would you like to meet W. C. Handy, who wrote 'St. Louis Blues'?" And I'd go with her to a party in Yonkers where a blind W. C. Handy was sitting in his wheelchair listening to Nat King Cole sing. Another time she brought me to a fancy apartment on the Upper West Side for the artist Jack Youngerman. I met a lot of young artists there, all standing up against a wall: Bob Rauschenberg, who became one of my best friends; Jasper Johns, who used to be very acerbic; Agnes Martin; Lenore Tawney, a tapestry artist; and Ray Johnson, who later killed himself.

Bob and I used to do some window displays for Bonwit Teller and Tiffany. But mostly I stuck to billboards. After General Outdoor Advertising, I graduated to Artkraft Strauss, which had all the billboarding in Times Square—the Palace billboard, Castro Convertible. I painted huge things, like the sign for the Astor and Victoria Theatres, 395 feet wide and fifty-eight feet high, and over one hundred different two-story-high Shenley whiskey bottles. I got so sick of painting those that after a while I wrote on the label "Mary had a little lamb its fleece was white as snow."

I eventually got sick, sick, sick of it all. The color and form were fun, but I wanted to do a new kind of artwork. At that time, the height of art in New York was Abstract Expressionism. Teachers would say to students, "Throw some paint on the canvas, make a mark, and then you have the obligation to make something out of it." After Pollock, I thought about how you can introduce imagery to get to nihilism again, and I came up with the idea of painting things so large that you couldn't recognize what they were. I had been painting billboards so close up, the imagery was in the back of my head instead of in front of me, and the billboards were really just pure color. That was the idea.

A few years after I arrived, I lived in an apartment

where Lincoln Center is now. It had a kitchen table, no chairs, no stove. On Thanksgiving Day, I was painting a Merry Christmas sign on top of a big billboard in Times Square, and I thought, son of a bitch, I'm tired of having turkey at the Automat alone for Thanksgiving. So I went and bought a big, frozen turkey. Then I called three girls I knew from the south and said, "You got a stove?" They said, "Yeah, we got a stove, but we don't have a pan!"

I called Wing Dong, a Chinese artist. I said, "Wing, I got three girls, a frozen turkey, and a stove, but I got no pan." He had a pan and offered to cook, and I insisted he stay for dinner. The franc was really low then, so you could get an exquisite bottle of French wine for ninety-nine cents. The boyfriends of two of the girls brought the wine, and we all had a big turkey dinner on the floor of their one-room apartment.

DAN RATHER

{ journalist
arrived: 1956 }

In the Texas of my youth, New York might as well have been Neptune. It was the stuff of children's stories. But it was the capital of the world, and I was damn sure not going to miss that.

The first time I went to New York—for two and a half days, when I was twenty-five—I hitchhiked from

Houston to Atlanta, where I then caught a Greydog (that is to say, a Greyhound bus) to New York. I stayed at the YMCA in Times Square, which was a good bit tattier and sleazier than I had anticipated. I was slack-jawed and wide-eyed. And a little bit scared, to be truthful about it. I was not a country boy; I had considered myself a big-city boy from Houston. I realized in Times Square what a rube I was.

But, boy, I wanted so much to go into one of those Times Square places with the bright lights. I saw a nice jazz joint that I now think was Birdland. I stood outside looking for a menu or something to tell me if they would charge for entering, because, frankly, it looked too expensive for me. I eventually just decided to open the door and take a step in. Smoke clung to the ceiling like draperies. A short man with a snap-brim hat and a cigar came up to me and said, "Check your hat and coat, sir." I was not prepared for that. So I stared at him for some time in silence and then mumbled, "Will it cost me anything?" He said, "No. I'm a fucking Chinese coolie." I got out of there, taking a bus to Philadelphia and hitchhiking the rest of the way back to Texas.

Although I visited New York many times since then—and took the train up from D.C. when I hosted the Sunday-night CBS news broadcast at eleven—my family and I didn't return to the city for good until 1979. We found a three-bedroom apartment on Seventy-second Street between Park and Madison. I remember my wife, Jean, said, "It's only $92,000." I blew a gasket. Let me get this straight: No lawn? No yard? And it's still $92,000? Well, Jean is by far the smartest of all the Rathers, and she explained to me that it was actually a good price. After we signed the papers, she said she wanted to renovate the kitchen for $50,000, and that we had to pay maintenance fees around $600 a month, which was like paying rent to live in a place you had supposedly bought. We argued a bit, but she prevailed in her great wisdom.

She was also smart enough to figure out that New York is never a megalopolis of however many millions; it's always just your neighborhood—the shoe repair guy, the carpenter, the grocer, the post office—like any small town in Texas, really. And everyone was so friendly; a neighbor welcomed us with an upside-down chocolate cake, which really impressed Jean because it is very difficult to make. She was a fan of tennis, and learned something in tennis that we took to heart for life in the city broadly. She told me, "When you play tennis in New York, you've gotta get your first serve in."

Like any immigrants, we had this Ellis Island mentality where we said we weren't going to give up our heritage and stop being Texans. Jean would tell the kids we were like Indians, and we had to go where the buffalo were; there's a hell of a lot of buffalo in New York. But it's odd, because New Yorkers and Texans get along so well. They have those same outsize personalities, that determination and passion, that "don't mess with me" quality. And they have the same law my maternal grandmother would tell me from the time I was a little boy: "If it is to be, it is up to me." Self-reliance, confidence. I really believe those lyrics, "If I can make it there, I'll make it anywhere."

In Texas, we have something we call "the Cortez moment," which refers to when the great Spanish explorer and conquistador of Mexico came and set up camp and then burned his boats. The phrase "burn

the boats" means there's nothing but forward, on-
ward, no turning back or running home scared. It's
a motto for New York as much as for Texas. When
you move here, if you're any good at all, you burn
the boats.

LARRY KRAMER

{ playwright }
arrived: 1957

After college I was stationed at Governors Island. We could come into New York every night if we wanted to, and God, we did. The USO gave out free theater tickets, and someone had donated two sixth-row-center tickets to the Metropolitan Opera. There weren't that many soldiers who wanted those tickets, so I went a lot to see Zinka Milanov and Antonietta

Stella. We had to wear our uniforms, but that was really fun.

I also got a chance to explore the gay bars off Third Avenue in Midtown. They all had men at the door who could tell if straight people were coming and wouldn't let them in. There was one bar in particular called the 316, on East Fifty-fourth. I would walk around the block five times before I got up the nerve to go in. There would be guys of all ages just getting off work. Everybody would stand around not talking to each other. There were unwritten regulations about cruising you had to learn. You didn't just go up and talk to somebody; you had to stare until they stared back.

After the army I got a job as a messenger boy in the mailroom of the William Morris Agency, where I made $39 a week. We were expected to survey the scene of whatever our interests were, so I went to see theater. I was also interested in becoming an actor myself, and I took classes with Sydney Pollack, who told me, "Larry, you're very good, but you'll never get the girl."

One of the great things about being in the mail-room was that you were encouraged to read everybody's mail. So I would stay late reading how much Elvis was making in Vegas, or who was going to get what part. But eventually enough was enough, and early one morning I marched into the office of my boss, Nat Lefkowitz. I said, "Mr. Lefkowitz, you don't know me from Adam. My name is Larry Kramer and I went to Yale and I think I'm smart enough not to be in the mailroom." You didn't do things like that, but that is, in fact, what you do if you want to impress someone. They transferred me out of the mailroom. They made me a secretary, and I had to learn shorthand.

TOMMY TUNE

{ director and choreographer

arrived: 1957 }

My graduation present from high school was a trip to New York, all the way from Texas. I was seventeen years old and got on the elevator at the Algonquin and there was the famous actress Anna May Wong. I went into my room starstruck. Then I lifted the window shade to look out, and there was a brick wall. It was the most romantic thing I'd ever seen. In Texas, you have sky. Here, a brick wall!

The shows on Broadway that season were incredible. Rosalind Russell in *Auntie Mame*, Rex Harrison and Julie Andrews in *My Fair Lady*. But the energy of the city was overwhelming. I went to the little coffee shop next door for breakfast, where everybody was swinging their nickels down on the counter and talking fast. I heard the person next to me say, "Coffee and corn." I wondered what that was. Corn on the cob for breakfast? But I didn't know what to order, so I said "Coffee and corn" too, and they brought me a corn muffin. Then I went to the Automat, which I thought was the coolest thing in the world because it looked like a food show—all this food behind glass. At the cafeteria they said, "Whaddya have, soup-er-juice?"

I panicked. "Uh, juice."

When they said "Orange-er-tomato?" it was so fast and so frightening that I just left my tray and went away.

I knew on that visit that I *had* to be in New York, that this is where I belonged, but I don't think I would have ever gotten up the nerve to come if it weren't for my friend Phillip Oesterman. He was a director who worked some in Houston and had a little apartment in New York. One day he pulled into my driveway and said, "Listen, I've been thinking. Here in Houston, if you dance and are talented and unusual, they call you a sissy or a weirdo. In New York, they call you a star. Let's go!"

I drove across the country with Phillip and slept on the couch of his West Side apartment. We arrived on Saint Patrick's Day. I remember there was a green stripe painted down the middle of Fifth Avenue, which I thought was a lucky omen. The trade papers listed an audition that very day for a touring company of *Irma La Douce*, and I went to sing "You've Gotta Have Heart." I remember the guys before me had such huge voices, I thought to myself, Tommy Tune, pack up your tap shoes and go back to Texas. But I got the job.

I think the light in the city was more golden back then. I loved Forty-second Street, and I didn't know it was a place where people accosted other people. I'd get hit on and not even realize it. One day I was walking through Greenwich Village, and this lady said, "Are you lost?" I told her I was looking for a grilled cheese sandwich, and she said, "Come up to my apartment, and I'll make you a grilled cheese sandwich." And she did.

DANIEL LIBESKIND

{ architect
arrived: 1959 }

I stood on the deck of the SS *Constitution*, hoping that would make America come quicker. The boat had started in Haifa, but we picked it up in Naples from Łódź, our hometown in Poland. When we got to New York, ours was one of the only families with all their luggage. Everyone else was crying about what had been lost.

It is a marvelous thing to see the New York skyline from the point of view of the short, flat water. It was an early morning in late August, and the sunlight was everywhere. It's not anything that anyone can imagine—a vision out of Dante's *Paradiso*.

I was thirteen, and I had won a scholarship to play my accordion. I would play in Town Hall with other gifted musicians (sometimes with Itzhak Perlman, who had also won a scholarship that year). I would get about $500 for a concert, and that was enough for my family to pay for rent, food, and laundry for a month. My father found a job working in a print shop downtown, and my mother worked in a sweatshop, but my accordion helped us very much.

We lived in the Bronx. It felt like home because it was one-third Yiddish, one-third Polish, and one-third broken English. I took an aptitude test for school, and since I knew zero English, I must have gotten a zero on it. They put me in a class for dummies—mostly girls who were learning how to type and be good secretaries. Even now I can type very well. But then everyone realized that we needed to beat the Russians and undo Sputnik and all of this, so I got put in Bronx High School of Science and exposed to mathematics and science. It was difficult. But in that situation you learn English overnight. I watched *The Twilight Zone, 77 Sunset Strip,* and *What's My Line?* on a television some neighbors had donated to us. And Superman cartoons.

Even though this was the 1960s, and I was a teenager, you must remember that I was a Polish Jew and very nerdy. The most illegal thing I did was buy a *Mad* magazine and hide it under my mattress from my parents. I know you are supposed to hide *Playboy*s when you are that age, but that was unimaginable. Day after day, I would be alone in MoMA and the Met, which for some reason were not that busy back then. I still have all these watercolors I did in the foyer of the Met with nobody in the foreground.

There was a great adventurous topography to New York—lots of things to do for free. A subway token cost only fifteen cents, so the adventure was accessible to everyone. Although I quickly learned that Manhattan was not really the city. It was a mecca for otherness: the rich, the tourists. We lived in true New York, in the Amalgamated Housing Cooperative near the Grand Concourse. True New Yorkers didn't have air conditioning; they sat on their stoop and talked with their neighbors and friends.

LIZA
MINNELLI

{ actress and singer
arrived: 1961 }

Bye Bye Birdie changed my mind. Until then I had wanted to be an ice-skater. But when I was fifteen, I went to New York with my parents, and Mama took me to a whole bunch of Broadway shows. I watched all those kids in *Bye Bye Birdie* looking so happy and having so much fun. So I asked my parents if I could take a summer in New York. They weren't so hot on that. "We'll talk about it later," they said. I asked them if they'd let me if I could get a job. "Well," they said, "I guess we're not going to stop you."

I did summer stock, winter stock, I moved scenery. I did any little thing. I just wanted to be part of theater, baby! I was instantly a gypsy, and I wore a gypsy robe, which was a rare thing for new people. I danced with all my beautiful dancer friends at the High School of Performing Arts, when it was still in Times Square. We'd spend all day dancing at Luigi's, and then talk all night at the Tripple Inn. We weren't old enough to drink, but we didn't need to. We'd have a Coke and just absorb the energy.

People wanted to go to clubs or parties; I just wanted to go to Sardi's. But I didn't have a dime. I lived in some bell-bottoms and a peacoat I bought from a place on Forty-second Street where the sailors went to get clothes—the real deal. I'd wake up, grab a Coke and a Hershey bar, and just get into it with this bright beautiful city. I would second-act it to the shows because I just couldn't afford them. But it was wonderful—you got to see all the best parts.

When I got my first apartment, on East Fifty-seventh Street, all I had in there was a rug, where I slept, and a mirror, for rehearsing. As I started to get roles, I treated myself to a portable record player and bought up every Tony Bennett record I could find. One day I was sitting on the rug and someone buzzes up and the doorman says, "Mr. Tony Bennett is here to see you." Couldn't be, I think—I tell him to quit joking. Ten seconds later it buzzes again, and this time it says, "Liza, it's Tony. I'm coming up." He comes in and I offer him a Coke and we sit on the rug for twenty minutes. I was just thrilled to pieces. He tells me, "You sing ballads better than you think." And I say that I can't sing, that I'm a dancer. But he got me thinking about it.

I had known Tony, of course. My childhood had been very special, but I didn't know that until I moved to New York. Growing up, they were just the neighbors' kids; it didn't matter that they were Bogey's kids. Candy Bergen, Mia Farrow, Natalie Wood—they were my girls. I babysat little Ronnie Howard, went on dates with little Christopher Walken. People are always coming to New York from forgotten, faraway places, and that's me too. Hollywood is a small, regimented town: my parents would wake up at six and be home by six. But in New York, everyone is so passionate all the time. I loved all that hurrying. I still love it. You always want more, and you want it now—bigger, brighter, better, more friends, more passion, more love, just more! It's how teenagers think. And I still think that way about the city, so I get to be a teenager my whole life. How's that! Not bad, baby.

NORA
EPHRON

{ writer and filmmaker
arrived: 1962 }

I moved to New York City the day I graduated from Wellesley. I'd found a job a week earlier by going to an employment agency on West Forty-second Street. I told the woman there that I wanted to be a journalist, and she said, "How would you like to work at *News-week*?" and I said fine. At the *Newsweek* interview I said I hoped to become a writer, and the man who interviewed me assured me that women weren't writers at *Newsweek*. It would never have crossed my mind to object, or to say, "You're going to turn out to be wrong about me." It was a given in those days that if you were a woman and you wanted to do certain things, you were going to have to be the exception to the rule. I was hired as a mail girl, for $55 a week.

I'd found an apartment with a friend from college at 110 Sullivan Street. The real estate broker assured us it was a coming neighborhood, on the verge of being red-hot. He was about twenty-five years off. Anyway, I packed up a rental car on graduation day and set off to New York. I got lost only once—I had no idea you weren't supposed to take the George Washington Bridge to get to Manhattan, so I had to pay the toll in both directions. I got to my apartment and discovered that the Feast of Saint Anthony was taking place on our block. There was no way to park—they were frying *zeppole* in front of my apartment—and actually, I was very excited about this. In some bizarre way, I thought that the street fair would be there for months, and that it would be sort of great and I could have all the cotton candy I ever wanted. Of course it was gone the next week.

The apartment on Sullivan Street was completely dreary, and I'm proud to say that was the last time I made the mistake of living in an apartment without any charm. Three months later I moved to West Forty-fourth Street between Ninth and Tenth with two other roommates. In those days people broke leases and moved all the time, it was no big deal. Apartments were cheap and available. The West Forty-fourth Street apartment was a parlor floor-through in a lovely brownstone with two fireplaces. It made no sense at all for three people to be living in it, but we had a wonderful year together. It was very *My Sister Eileen*. Not that we had seen or read *My Sister Eileen*. Then one of my roommates got married and the other went back to Venezuela, so I moved to a fifth-floor walk-up in Chelsea.

My job at *Newsweek* couldn't have been more prosaic, but luckily I was the Elliott girl—the mail girl who worked directly for the magazine's editor, Osborn Elliott. This meant I got to work late on Friday nights as they closed the magazine, and I got to read all the first drafts the writers wrote and the corrected drafts coming back from the editors. It was actually interesting, and in the tradition of all such places, we thought that the entire world was on tenterhooks waiting for the next edition.

A few weeks after I moved to New York, I met Victor Navasky. He was editing a satiric magazine called *Monocle*, and although the magazine came out only rarely, it had a lot of parties. Through Victor I met a huge number of people who became friends for life. Then, in December, the famous 114-day newspaper lockout began, and Victor got some money to put out parodies of the *New York Post* and the *New York Daily News*. I did a parody of Leonard Lyons's gossip column, and the *Post* offered me a tryout for a reporting job. I was hired after a week, and I couldn't believe it: I felt that I'd achieved my life's ambition, and I was only twenty-one. Of course, once you get what you want, you eventually want something else, but all I wanted right then was to be a newspaper reporter and I was.

I'd known since I was five, when my parents forced me to move to California, that I was going to live in New York eventually, and that everything in between was just a horrible intermission. I'd spent those sixteen years imagining what New York was going to be like. I thought it was going to be the most exciting, magical, fraught-with-possibility place that you could ever live in; a place where if you really wanted something, you might be able to get it; a place where I'd be surrounded by people I was dying to be with. And I turned out to be right.

TOM WOLFE

{ writer
arrived: 1962 }

I'd been on campuses for ten straight years, and it was just awful. When I was at Yale I used to go down to Chapel Street at 10:00 pm, when the *New York Daily News* came in. I was gradually getting hooked on newspapers, so after my last year of grad school I went to New York and applied to the *Daily News*. They offered me a job as a copyboy that paid $40 a week, which even then was miserable. I considered taking it until I heard someone laughing. When I asked what was so funny, he told me they had never had a PhD copyboy before. And I could see what the next few years would be like: "Hey, Doc, go get me some coffee."

So I sent my résumé out to fifty newspapers and spent six years working for the *Springfield Union* and the *Washington Post*. It wasn't until 1962 that I got a job worth having in New York: working for the *Herald Tribune*. There was a party for me the night before I left D.C., and I stayed out much too late. In fact, I caught the last bus of the night. I arrived in New York City at four in the morning feeling very romantic. I raised my fist—"I'm going to conquer you yet!"— the way Eugène de Rastignac does in Balzac's *Le Père Goriot*. I was all alone, so I had breakfast at an Automat across the street from my hotel. All the food was yellow: the eggs, the coffee, even the meat.

I then headed off to the *Tribune*, just off Times Square, feeling more romantic the closer I got to the paper. Suddenly I heard this voice. "T.K.!" Those were my first two initials—Thomas Kennerly. It was an old girlfriend, and she said, "How would you like to come to a party tonight?" The party was on Central Park

West, at an apartment that belonged to the poet Robert Lowell, who had arranged a summer apartment trade with people from Brazil. There were these Brazilians, and the party was nice, maybe only twenty of us there. All of a sudden the host said, "Gilberto, can't you play something for us?" and the musicians started playing "The Girl from Ipanema."

This destroyed my whole fantasy, which was to come to New York alone, ready to take on the city. I wanted to be a romantic figure, but Christ, it was over that first day: meeting an old friend, going to an incredibly cosmopolitan party. Over the next few months, I discovered how unromantic the things I had once found romantic were. Being on packed subways became a real nuisance. I would be walking down the street and a gust of wind would blow a grimy newspaper around my leg. I remember seeing so many stars of movies and music walking down the street. That was exciting, until it dawned on me that these people have to live *somewhere*.

But it was a much safer city back then, before the late 1960s. I took the subway everywhere and never thought twice about it being dangerous, whether I was going to the Bronx or the Rockaways. I was on the

2:00 pm to 10:00 pm shift, which I liked very much. The disappointing thing about newspapers at the time was that so many reporters lived in the suburbs, so there was this mad race to Grand Central Terminal at 11:00 pm. But I'd get off work and be ready to do something. There was a place on Seventh Avenue where you could get dinner at three in the morning. It was called something like Mamma Margherita— a real Italian name with wonderful waitresses who treated you like they were your mothers.

I do remember taking a taxi one night at two in the morning, when I'd been here a matter of months. I was heading to my place on Gramercy Park with $1.01 in my pocket, all in change with only one quarter. I knew I wouldn't make it to Gramercy in a cab, so I told myself I'd let the meter go up to eighty-five cents, at which point I'd have enough for a tip and could walk the rest of the way. So it go up to eighty-five cents, but I wasn't quick enough to tell the cabbie to stop. It went up to ninety cents. I thought, well, that's so bad I might as well go to a dollar. When I got out I handed him all the change and walked west on Fortieth in the direction I knew the cabbie couldn't go. The next thing I knew, I heard this car going at high speed up the block the wrong direction. It was the cab driver, of course. He stopped beside me and said, "Hey sport, you gave me a penny too much!" At which point he threw all the change at me. I remember looking around in the dark until I saw the quarter. I picked it up and walked home.

JUDY COLLINS

{ singer
arrived: 1963 }

I was twenty-three and just out of the hospital in Colorado, where I'd been recovering from TB for five months. I don't know how I got it—probably from working too hard, running from one club to another. I left the hospital to go to Washington and sing for President Kennedy at the B'nai B'rith celebration, and then it was straight to New York.

My apartment was on West Tenth and Hudson—a one-minute walk to the Gaslight, the Bitter End, and the Village Gate. I immediately rented a grand piano, and my ex-husband sent me my skis, clothes, and some of our wedding china. The piano was the main attraction, of course. I didn't have a lot of work right away, so I would go to the antique shops. I found a fantastic mirror that I spent weeks refinishing, and a $35 set of drawers with a beautiful marble top that I still own.

The Village was like a small town. Izzy Young's Folklore Center was the place to buy finger picks and copies of *Sing Out!*, and to find out where everyone was playing. My five-year-old son was in town a lot, and he loved music, so we'd go to Washington Square Park. I didn't like carrying my guitar around much, but I'd usually find a banjo or guitar player there and sing with them. I was about a third of the way to being famous, so most of them didn't know who I was.

Those days I wore long, dangly silver earrings, high-heeled boots, and a lot of leather. I bought my clothes from shops in the Village: a wraparound denim skirt, long flowered dresses, Romanian blouses

tied in the front, Mexican wedding dresses. I'd start
my days with a lot of coffee and a meeting with my
manager or with the people at Elektra. For lunch
I'd go to the Kettle of Fish with Walter Raim, who
had produced my second album, and we'd have a big
shrimp salad and maybe some iced tea (I wasn't yet
drinking during the day). At night, I'd get together
with friends—Lily Tomlin and Jane Wagner, Leonard
Cohen and Joan Baez—and we'd make dinner, drink
wine, and play music, or Art D'Lugoff would let us in
to the Village Gate.

My most vivid memory of that time was on the
twelfth of April, when I went to see a Dylan concert
at Town Hall. I had seen him live before, but he was
schlubby and had sung nothing but Woody Guthrie.
In person he was shy and brainy. But his first solo
concert—that one blew me away. After that show, I
went backstage to hang out with him and Jac Holz-
man. I told him I wanted to do "Masters of War" on
my next album.

I was working like a tiger to grow my career. (I
was becoming Judy Collins, and that was quite an effort.) But I was miserable. Even though it was thrilling

to be doing what I was doing, I had depression and didn't know what was the matter. I drank too much, but everyone in that milieu drank too much. One day I called a doctor and said I thought I was being poisoned; that was my default opinion when I got depressed. He put me on Miltown, and of course within two months of getting to New York I was in therapy.

DANNY DeVito

{ actor
arrived: 1963 }

Growing up in Asbury Park, New Jersey, I always
wanted a New York license plate. It was one of those
things that felt so cool. Our grandmother lived in
Flatbush, and we'd visit her every weekend, driving
up through Staten Island and over the ferry. I remember the really good salted pretzels, and the little wax
cups of Medix orange juice. Sometimes we'd go to

Ferrara's down in Little Italy and buy a whole bunch of Italian cake.

I didn't move to New York until I was nineteen and commuting to the American Academy of Dramatic Arts. The drive got to be too much, so I decided to bite the bullet and stay with my aunt. Every day I would catch a couple of buses and get to the Nostrand Avenue subway stop, trying with all my might to get past the doughnut shops. They had these cinnamon doughnuts, and they used to blow the smell out onto the station. It was amazing. But you know, we all have hero's journeys in life. One of mine was getting by the doughnuts.

I was a hippie kid, with a little bit of beatnik in me, too. I was a vegetarian with long hair. I did yoga. I was always wearing T-shirts and sweatshirts. I just wanted to dig in and become part of the cement and the bricks and the buildings of the city. I had a particular affinity for the Bowery, which was lined with rows of people sleeping on the streets. The grittiness of the city wasn't frightening. I thought it was really cool.

Someone did try to mug me once at Fourth Street and Sixth Avenue, but it didn't work. I intellectualized the situation. He had a kitchen knife, and I started talking: "I realize that you have no money, and maybe your tampering with drugs forced you into this situation, and I have no money to speak of either because I'm working as an actor. Why would you want to stick this big knife in my throat? With all due respect, we're all in it together. I mean, I have empathy for you, you have empathy for me. . . ." By the time I stopped blabbing we were at Sheridan Square, with people selling papers and cops getting coffee. He put the knife back in his pants and went his way.

That first summer, I did a play at the Eugene O'Neill Theater in Connecticut, where I met Michael Douglas. We came back to New York, and I immediately moved into his apartment on West Eighty-ninth Street. It was one big room, and I slept on the floor. But you know, we were hippies; we didn't even think about going to sleep. It was called *crashing*. We'd hang out with John Guare and with John Noonan and a couple of guys who weren't named John. Most of the experiences that Michael and I had we've never been able to talk about. It's terrible! But I had a rule: If he was coming home with a girl, he had to bring another one too, or he wasn't allowed in.

LAUREN
HUTTON

{ model and actress
arrived: 1964 }

I came to New York for two things: to get to Africa and to find LSD. In those days it was legal. You could get it from this Swiss chemical company, and I met six guys who were very willing to give it to me. But I didn't like any of them enough to accept, so it took me a few months. As for Africa, I was supposed to meet a friend in New York, and we were going to take a tramp steamer to Tangier. It was going to cost $140. Once I got there, my plan was to take a bus for ten cents to the outskirts of town and see elephants and rhinoceroses and giraffes. I was as ignorant as a telephone pole.

In any case, the friend didn't show up. I don't think I ever found out what happened to her. I waited for two hours at Idlewild and then took a bus to the Port Authority. I was going through the bus terminal, and I was twenty-one and these very strangely dressed young black guys were following me and saying these weird things. And I thought, Uh-oh. I didn't realize they were pimps, but I knew it was bad. So I panicked and got into a cab. When the cabbie asked me where to go, I didn't know. Then I remembered Tiffany's. I'd heard of Tiffany's. And I knew the corner of Fifty-seventh and Fifth. So I said, "Fifty-seventh and Fifth! Tiffany's!"

It was very early Sunday, and when I got out, New York was deserted. No one anywhere. I had to figure out who I knew and get to a phone. I started bawling as I was walking down the street. Everything I'd ever owned—old college test papers, sneakers from high school—was in these two suitcases. And I couldn't walk with them. I'd bring one bag about six feet up, and then I'd go back and get the other bag and bring it six feet up. Humping these suitcases down Fifth Avenue. And then I got to a phone booth, this box of glass and metal, and I think I felt protected. I just sat there for a while and cried and tried to figure it out. And then I remembered another friend from New Orleans who was supposed to be in New York. She told me to come right over.

She had this wonderful boyfriend from Brooklyn who said, "Well, you're going to have to get a job." It made sense; I was going to Africa! There was an ad in the *New York Times* that said, "Wanted: High-fashion model for Christian Dior. Must have experience." He said, "This! You could do this!" And I said, "No, no. I've never been a model." And he looked dead straight at me and said, "Of. Course. You. Have." So I was getting all kinds of lessons in New Yorkese and survival, the very morning I got in.

CHUCK CLOSE

{ artist
arrived: 1967 }

I paid $150 a month for a raw loft on Greene Street, and all my friends who were already living here laughed, thinking it was outrageous to pay that much. The loft had no heat. I painted for an entire year with gloves on and just my trigger finger sticking out to the button on the airbrush. Literally, the coffee would freeze in its mug; the toilet would freeze overnight. We slept under a pile of blankets.

SoHo was rats and rags and garbage trucks: there were occasional wars between one Mafia-owned waste-management company and another, during which one would burn the other's trucks. There might have been twenty artists—or people of any kind—living between Houston and Canal; you could have shot a cannon down Greene Street and never hit anybody. But we all lived within a few blocks of each other: Brice Marden, Richard Serra, Nancy Graves, Phil Glass. We were in someone's loft every night, either listening to a composer like Steve Reich or watching dancers like Yvonne Rainer and Trisha Brown. A lot of us helped Richard make his lead prop pieces, because he needed muscle and brawn to roll the lead and stack it up. Phil was his only paid assistant, and the rest of us were this group of writers, filmmakers, even Spalding Gray. After work we'd go over to this cafeteria in what is now the Odeon, and we'd sit around and dream up ideas on the back of napkins.

One of my classmates at Yale had become a dean at the School of Visual Arts, and he hired a bunch of us to teach. SVA was crazy. The director, Silas Rhodes, had a policy of never failing students so they wouldn't be drafted. This meant that no student could ever be too bad or use too many drugs, so it was like teaching in Bangladesh or something—burned-out carcasses of speed freaks littered the hallways. But then the faculty was so busy revolting that there was little differentiation between them and the students. It was all revolt, all the time.

We didn't feel we had anything much to teach, anyway. But I do remember a course called Survival. If you wanted to live in a loft, you had to learn how to put up your own drywall, insulate the ceiling, and figure out some way to heat it. So one week we brought in a plumber, the next week an electrician. They'd teach real bare-bones stuff, but it took the scariness out of living in New York.

Sometimes we'd go to the Exploding Plastic Inevitable, Andy Warhol's nightclub extravaganza that he ran on St. Marks Place. But the main thing was the watering holes, chief among them Mickey Ruskin's Max's Kansas City. Andy and his entourage would be in the back room with Rauschenberg and his entourage, and we younger artists like Robert Smithson and Dorothea Rockburne and Mel Bochner would tend to be in booths up front. There would be huge fights. At the time, there were only about fourteen contemporary art galleries, so you could start a Saturday at Eighty-sixth Street and work your way down Madison to see every piece of contemporary art being shown in New York. Usually someone would have done that and then come in Max's and say, "I just saw so-and-so's show and it's great," and then everyone would put him on the spot to explain why it was great, and they'd become more and more aggressive, and sometimes they would freak out, throw a drink, and walk out.

There was music upstairs—Janis Joplin would be leaning up against the jukebox with a bottle of Southern Comfort, singing along with Edith Piaf with tears streaming down her cheeks. Mickey would trade artists' work for a tab, so there was a big John Chamberlain sculpture in the front—a huge galvanized piece that was the coatrack for the whole place. Along one wall was a really beautiful Donald Judd, and in the corner in the back room was a red Dan Flavin that put a particularly eerie hue on top of all the pale Warhol Superstars.

ANDRÉ ACIMAN

{ writer
arrived: 1968 }

Summer of '68. Europe's gone mad. From April through July, riots break all over Germany, then France and Italy. The Russians invade Czechoslovakia. That same August, as I'm preparing to step on American soil for the first time, violent images from the Chicago Democratic National Convention tell me that what I've just seen in Europe awaits me in the States.

I am filled with strange misgivings and fears. Earlier in spring Bobby Kennedy and Martin Luther King Jr. were assassinated, the War in Vietnam still rages, Columbia students have just rioted, and Richard Nixon will most likely become president. The world is not a good place. I am almost eighteen. I could be drafted within months of landing in the United States.

In September, my uncle picks me up at JFK and says, "Welcome home." This, my home? I ask myself with dismay and disbelief as we zip through the huge airport. Unlike those who arrived in America a century ago, there is no time for gaping starry-eyed at the Statue of Liberty from aboard the packed decks of giant ocean liners; there is no Statue of Liberty at JFK, no Ellis Island to be quarantined in as you learn to close the ledger on the Old World and take baby steps into the new. I want to be locked in a time capsule and be shielded from the present.

Through the smog, the looming silhouette of Manhattan's skyscrapers flutters ominously, so distant, so unreal, just as I want it to be. I want everything to be unreal, I am not here, I am not ready to be here. Projects, trellised bridges, ugly bridges, fire escapes everywhere as we speed up the highway to the Bronx.

My uncle takes a few minutes to show me the Grand Concourse, where he used to live, the boulevard of dreams. What grandeur, he says as he races up the Concourse. What drab buildings, I think. I am definitely not here.

In the home where my aunt and he have put me up, I'm surrounded by strange scents—a blend of Pine-Sol, Dial soap, cedar, mothballs, and lemon Pledge to buff the wood paneling downstairs. At night, the faux wood creaks, my clothes smell of cedar and of wood polish; then to offset the scent of faux pine and faux lemon, I find myself smelling of Dial soap. I don't want to smell of Dial soap. Everything is faux: the smell of bread; the juices; even the weather these days is faux summer, called Indian summer. In all this, the one thing I recognize and find comfort in is a song that had already come out in Europe and is on radio stations everywhere in New York: "Hey Jude." In the wood-paneled basement, which is temporarily my room, "Hey Jude" takes me back to happier days in Rome, when on long walks alone I'd try to imagine the unimaginable as I waited for a visa I kept hoping might never come.

When the visa finally does arrive, it is already too

late for college. My uncle says he'll fix this, *You watch*. He'll sweet-talk the woman at the registrar's office and get me to register for courses, even if I'm three weeks late, *You watch*. He drives me to Lehman College, known at the time as Hunter College, in the Bronx. The lady at the registrar, who adamantly refuses to let me register so late, says I'll just have to wait till the spring term. Meanwhile, what are your plans? she asks. I mutter something tame and docile about plans I don't have. Yes, intervenes my uncle, but can't she make an exception? None whatsoever. What will he do for five months, twiddle his thumbs? She ignores the question.

Did you see how ugly she is? says my uncle as soon as we leave her office. There is something refreshing and almost reassuringly Old World in this sort of remark; it brings admissions officers, bureaucrats, universities, my future career, my entire life in America, down to a plain, petty, ordinary, human scale. As we walk out of the building, I spot about two hundred students lounging about on the grass. I know I'll never be one of them, long-haired hippies with guitars, their books and notebooks littered all over, many of the men shirtless, the women barefoot, some necking. I

ANDRÉ ACIMAN 89

am wearing flannel pants, a buttoned shirt, a necktie, and polished brown shoes—to make a good impression, my uncle had said. I look ridiculous. You should have said something, he says as he steps into the car. He's right; I should have said something. This is America, we speak up here.

My uncle is visibly upset. He is a busy-busy man. I had better get busy too and find myself a job. No twiddling thumbs, young man. A few days later he puts me on the subway at Gun Hill Road in the Bronx and tells me to change at Fifty-ninth Street and get off at Fifty-first Street. There I'll find an employment agency on Lexington Avenue; they'll help me land a job. It's ten o'clock when I arrive at the agency. By lunchtime, I have already been to an interview, where I'm told that I shouldn't be applying for a mailroom position. Several dimes and many phone calls later, I manage to arrange for an interview at four o'clock. Meanwhile I've walked all around Midtown Manhattan. I've seen Park Avenue. Fifth Avenue too, caught a glimpse of the Empire State Building. I've had lunch at a place called Chock Full o'Nuts. I've even found time to walk into the Rizzoli bookshop because I am already homesick.

By late afternoon, though, I am lucky, and I've landed a job at Lincoln Center at a salary of $75 a week. I start in a few days. This is totally new. I've never earned money before. I'm struggling to contain the strange and unexpected feeling of lightness and bliss that suddenly takes hold of me. On Broadway, I feel as though I've been let into something welcoming, huge, munificent. Even the scowling statue of Columbus, which turned its back to me as soon as I'd seen it, looks different now, wants to know me better, wishes me well—So you're one of us now! My aunt and uncle are happy for me. "Hop on the train and come home!" I don't want to tell her that I want to hang out awhile—feel the city, walk the city, open up to a city I've been trying my best to stave off.

I decide not to head back to the East Side but to walk up Broadway. It's five in the afternoon, and the cast of light on this late Indian summer afternoon glistens on the side of buildings facing west. This, I can tell by staring at my subway map, is Central Park. So this must be Broadway. And then, for the first time, I finally glimpse the whole of Lincoln Center, majestic, posh, irreducibly modern. I have never before, even in Europe, seen so immense an institution devoted to one thing only: Art. And I'm going to be its youngest mail boy, I think, chuckling to myself. When I scan the billboards, Art, it seems, is more at home here than it has been anywhere else in the world. I don't want to believe this, or not quite yet, but I already feel that there is as much old stuff here as there is new. The blending of the two enthralls me.

Beyond Lincoln Center lies the Seventy-second Street station, where I'm to take the subway to the Bronx. I have time still. Once on Seventy-second Street, I decide that this walk is long overdue and that rather than disturb the mood I'm in, I'll walk up to the Seventy-ninth local station. This is the first time I'm alone in the New World, and I love the New World, its new buildings, its old buildings, its fruit vendors, its large banks, its tiny parks where old folk sit on long benches, its buses, its eddy of cabs, its windows that tell me there's a whole way of life behind each one that I wouldn't know the first thing about but am dying to peer into. I can sense this is exactly the New York I'd been dreaming of but was afraid to go looking for because I feared it existed only in Leonard Bernstein and in Billy Wilder's films— not the East Side, not the Bronx, not Queens, but a narrow strip whose name, as I would find out soon enough, is the Upper West Side.

For the next five months, until the start of college, I take this walk almost every evening, starting on Fifty-ninth Street and going all the way up Broadway to Columbia University, passing by Dante Park, Verdi Square, Straus Park, nodding at one movie theater after the other along the way, thinking of all the films I am craving to see—*2001: A Space Odyssey*, *The Odd Couple*, *Romeo and Juliet*—already sensing that as I walk an improvised ritual blossoms between me and the city, and that this must be the stuff of magic and love.

This is your walk and this is your moment and this is your time capsule, says the city every evening as I leave the mailroom and step outside to find the lights of Lincoln Square. This is the moment when you can take me and mold me and make me in your image, and I'll be what you wish and I'll take after all your wants and whims, I'll woo you if I have to till you get used to me and love me. But after this I'll harden into what you see now and what you want now, and I may never change again. Buildings will come and go, and today's movie theaters will be gone soon enough, you will grow older too, but come the evening of every day, you'll find me as you find me now, waiting for you to step out into the speckled evening to recall, once again, as ever again, that you and I are of one kind. This is your New York.

MARY BOONE

{ art gallerist

arrived: 1970 }

I remember that the first exhibition I was part of was by Chuck Close, and that he sat in my office during the opening listening to the World Series. That was at Klaus Kertess's gallery, the Bykert Gallery. Lynda Benglis, who was my teacher at Hunter College, said, "Oh, if you need a job, my boyfriend owns a gallery." Because I thought I was going to come here and work at a museum, but I did that, and it really seemed so lifeless.

Klaus closed the gallery after ten years because it was getting to be too successful! He said it was too much of a business. It's so different now. In the early days I remember Brice Marden had seven one-person shows and never sold a painting. Even when I showed Julian Schnabel, it took me two years to sell the first painting.

Julian was the first artist to leave my gallery, and I was heartbroken. It was like the spring of 1984, and I was sitting in my office, crying. In his explanation at the time—you know, it's like anything, probably things change with the telling every time. But in those days, what he said was that he wanted to be separated. He said, "How many artists do you have in the Carnegie International?" And it was basically the whole gallery. And he said, "Well, if I go to Pace, I'm the only artist from that gallery in the Carnegie." He wanted a kind of separateness from me, but also from his generation. He wanted to be seen as an individual. We're still good friends; I think he's a fantastic filmmaker. I also have a different perception of this, because I think that life is about shared experiences, and if you have an experience with an artist, you never lose that. It's like if you're married and you have a child with somebody, you're never, ever really separated. And the child is the art. So anyway, I was sitting in my office crying, and Jean-Michel Basquiat comes in. And he was so sweet! He was so upset I was sitting there crying. He put his arms around me, and he said, "Mary, don't worry. I'm gonna be much more famous than Julian." And then he walked out, and he came back in with a huge watermelon, which he plunked on my desk, and we ate.

DIANE VON FURSTENBERG

{ designer
arrived: 1970 }

I was twenty-two years old and had just gotten married to Prince Egon von Furstenberg. I was pregnant and carrying a big suitcase of stencils I was hoping to sell in America. I decided that instead of flying, I wanted to come very slowly in order to think about my future. So I took a boat. I arrived in October, so it was New York at its best—that beautiful blue crisp. Coming from Europe, I had expected the city would look modern, and actually, it didn't. I was a young princess, so I lived on Park Avenue and had some small children and blah blah blah. But we were a young couple, and fairly good looking with a nice title, so we were invited everywhere. We would see Andy Warhol, Halston, Diana Vreeland, Giorgio Sant'Angelo, and, of course, lots of Europeans. It was a movable feast: Gino's and Elaine's and La Grenouille. And I threw many dinner parties. What I remember clearly is that you could go to the supermarket and for $50 you could buy pasta, salad, and a big ham.

PADMA LAKSHMI

{ television host

arrived: 1974 }

I first came to New York on Halloween night. I was four years old and flew on Air India's unaccompanied-minor program. I remember landing, and seeing all the big buildings, and being superexcited about this new adventure, and also, of course, being reunited with my mother. She was waiting there to pick me up.

There weren't that many Indian groceries in Manhattan back then, so my mother would take me on little field trips: to Jackson Heights for Indian spices, to Chinatown for noodles and Asian vegetables, to Spanish Harlem to eat empanadas or find sugarcane and tamarind. She wanted to introduce my young palate to all types of flavors and cuisines and ingredients. She didn't want me to be left out at school, and she wanted me to be able to eat everywhere.

My mother worked at Sloan-Kettering, and we lived in subsidized housing on the Upper East Side. I remember roller-skating down from Eighty-first Street and meeting her for lunch in the summers. We'd eat falafel from a pushcart on First Avenue. Looking back, I'm amazed how much we ate street food. My perfect meal would be a pretzel with mustard and then an Italian ice. I was a vegetarian for a lot of my childhood, so I would order a hot dog but tell the vendor to leave the hot dog out—just the bun and the fixings, like sauerkraut and mustard and relish. Slowly I started eating hot dogs.

LORNE MICHAELS

{ television producer }

arrived: 1975

I'd been living in California for the better part of five years, and what I remember most about the transition to 30 Rock is that I didn't have the required clothes. You know, when I was writing for *Laugh-In*, we worked in a motel and wore Hawaiian shirts and pants that flared. I remember going to Saks Fifth Avenue and buying an oxblood-colored V-neck sweater, and then buying a green corduroy jacket on Madison Avenue. I could wear the jacket with jeans, which then was a relatively fresh style. I was twenty-nine turning thirty, and I felt invincible.

There wasn't much television being done in New York—and the shows that were still here were soaps. The crew who knew how to put on a live show were still around, but they hadn't done it since the industry had moved to California. To do *Saturday Night Live*, it was like we were putting new wine in old television shows.

But when I walked into the lobby of Rockefeller Center the first time, I thought, Well, this show is absolutely going to work. There's something about walking into 30 Rock that puts audiences in a good mood. There was so much available space at the time, it was like there were deer running through the hall. And most of us who worked on the show didn't mind spending so much time in the office—30 Rock was nicer than our apartments. It felt as if we were on an adventure, tapping into an older tradition.

I met a lot of people right away, and each would show me a different part of the city. Michael O'Donoghue and Anne Beatts wanted me for drinks at the Oyster Bar. Herb Sargent, who came on board to do Weekend Update, took me to Elaine's. Candice Bergen and I went to the Russian Tea Room. But the first and deepest friendship I made that summer was with Paul Simon. We would go to this restaurant called Chin-Ya in the Woodward Hotel, and I would bounce ideas off him as I started to put the show together in my mind.

CINDY
SHERMAN

{ artist
arrived: 1977 }

It was the summer of 1977, and I was terrified of the city. Son of Sam was going around murdering couples, the city blacked out for twenty-four hours, the transit strike stopped all the buses, and all of a sudden women who used to wear little pumps to work now started wearing sneakers. I don't remember leaving the apartment much. I was just like, "Oh my God, here I am in the city!"

There were a ton of deserted old buildings in New York, and it was just a matter of finding one that someone would let you move into, and that you could turn into something habitable. The first place I lived in was a sublet from an artist friend on Gold and Fulton streets. It was just one room with a toilet down the hall and a shower that hooked up to the sink in the room. There was some printing company on my floor, and I'd be sharing the toilet with these old-time guys who'd been working there for forty years. My kitchen was just a fridge, two hot plates, and a toaster oven. I think we were all there illegally, because sometimes people would make really elaborate systems of hiding the bed and the kitchen.

By five o'clock the neighborhood would be deserted, but Robert Longo, Nancy Dwyer, Michael Zwack, Eric Bogosian, and I would go to clubs like the Mudd Club and Tier 3, where punk new-wave bands would play. The scene then was all about artists who were also musicians who were also filmmakers. Sometimes it was about finding a band that was just good to dance to. I remember being at the Mudd Club when the B-52s played, and there were only ten of us in the audience, dancing right in front of the stage. Then we'd head to the twenty-four-hour diner on Broadway and Canal Street called Dave's and get egg creams.

The first New York job I got was at Macy's, and I hated it so much I quit after one day. I wanted to work in the cosmetics department—I was interested in makeup—but their personnel screening placed me as the assistant-assistant-assistant buyer to the bathrobe department. It was just so horrible, in some window-less part of the building. After Macy's I worked in the afternoons as a receptionist at a gallery called Artist Space on Franklin and Hudson for $80 a week. Nancy worked at Barnes & Noble. We all wanted to make art, but I don't think any of us expected to live off our work. We mostly showed at alternative galleries where nobody bought anything, and we didn't expect other-wise. If you did sell something, it was such a treat, such a shock, that somebody would buy it.

When I was a teenager in Long Island, I'd come into the city once in a while with some girlfriends, and all we would do is go to Macy's and try on clothes. And when I was in college I would dress up in public and be in character (like, say, a pregnant woman) at an opening or a party. I tried that in New York a couple of times at my receptionist job. Once I went to work as a nurse. And another time as a secretary from the 1950s. I sort of fit in because I was sitting in front of the desk, and I'd be like, "What would you like? What do you need?" But it gave me the creeps to do it in New York, I think because I felt too vulnerable.

JANN WENNER

{ magazine editor
arrived: 1977 }

When *Rolling Stone* decided to move our headquarters from San Francisco, we settled on 745 Fifth Avenue, at the corner of the Plaza, with a wraparound terrace overlooking Central Park. If you're going to move across the country, why not move to the heart of the city?

We were the first new thing to move into New York in years. Everyone was fleeing. Corporate headquarters were moving to Connecticut and Westchester. So we had a big party at the MoMA sculpture garden, and Mayor Beame gave us the key to the city. President Ford came by because his son Jack was working for us. Jackie Onassis couldn't have been more gracious. She'd have dinner parties at her house, and invite people she wanted to introduce us to. Literary types like Pete Hamill and Mike Nichols I remember distinctly.

The people we knew were on the East Side. Jane and I sublet and then bought a fantastic duplex on Sixty-sixth Street and Lexington that belonged to Piedie Gimbel, who I met through Dick Goodwin. I had a regular table at the café bar at the Sherry-Netherland, where I ate lunch almost every day. The city was smaller then, and we all felt part of this generational renewal of spirit. *Saturday Night Live* was just getting started, and we all hung out together, operating almost in tandem. Norman Mailer had moved back to New York. We had Andy Warhol do a big portrait of Bella Abzug for the cover of our "Welcome to New York" issue, and a few months later got Tom Wolfe starting to imagine *Bonfire of the Vanities*. It was an era of parties, and a great time for drugs and alcohol. Elaine's was thriving. We felt more than welcomed. New York loves ambitious people—eats them up.

GRAYDON CARTER

{ magazine editor

arrived: 1978 }

When you first approach New York City by car from the north, the signs directing you to the actual island of Manhattan are small and easy to miss. I was twenty-nine and driving down from Ottawa, and I did almost exactly what Sherman McCoy did. I took a wrong turn and wound up in the Bronx. I stopped at a McDonald's and got directions and somehow managed to get safely into the city.

I had seen an ad in the *New York Times* for the Prince George Hotel on Twenty-eighth Street. It was slightly raffish—I mean there were police in the lobby most nights—but you could see the place once had great bones. My room had a bed, a dresser, and an old television set with rabbit ears. And no phone. It had a student rate of $22 a night. The trouble was, I couldn't go to work in a suit and tie and still get the student rate, so I had to dress like a student in the morning, go downstairs to settle the bill for the previous night in cash, and take my suit with me to work.

I had landed a job as a writer in the business section at *Time* magazine, which in those days was considered one of the plum places in journalism. On my first day, I got in Monday morning at 8:00 am sharp. Unfortunately, nobody told me that the writers and editors, having put in late hours on Thursday and Friday, didn't show up Mondays until noon. So I had about four hours to cool my heels. I bought some papers and went down to the wonderful old coffee shop in the bowels of the Time & Life Building, that had a long, snaky counter and waitresses with those little Dutch hats and white aprons. I hit it off with one of the luncheonette waitresses, who was older, and clearly took pity on me, and always tried to get me a stool in her working area.

When I returned, I was taken around the writers' offices and was introduced to, among others, Walter Isaacson and Jim Kelly. Libby Waite who was the secretary for Assistant Managing Editor Ed Jamieson, thought Jim, who had started a week earlier, and I should get to know each other. And so the next week we went off to the East River Savings Bank in Rockefeller Center, where we opened bank accounts and then across the street to have lunch at Charley O's. Libby had a good eye. Jim and I have been friends since, and were best men at each other's wedding.

Writers in those days typed on huge Underwood upright typewriters with five sheets of carbon paper separating the canary yellow copy paper. When stories were done we separated each of the copies and sent them by pneumatic tube to the editors who needed to see them. The work was put into the system and in a few hours, a formal manuscript came back with the disheartening stamp "WRITER'S VERSION."

As writers we were encouraged not to do any actual

reporting—that was done by correspondents. While they were out in all corners of the globe reporting and filing early in the week, we slipped off for lunches at Chez Napoléon or Tout Va Bien, two gloriously quaint French restaurants in the West Fifties that are still in business. It would be the rare lunch when two of us wouldn't polish off at least a bottle of wine. Everybody smoked: in offices, in hallways, in elevators. *Everywhere.*

In the evening, when I was waiting for my story to come back from the editor or fact-checking, I'd use the long distance phone line to call home, and then go down to the morgue, and sift through the files. *Time* maintained clipping files on everything and everybody. Presidents and ex-presidents got their own individual rooms. Every newspaper or magazine story had been carefully cut out, stamped, and clipped together. I remember finding the business card for Fred Waldo Demara Jr., the great imposter, in his file. And I came across a 1935 letter Condé Nast had written to Henry Luce informing him that he was folding *Vanity Fair* into *Vogue.*

Talent was thick on the ground at *Time* in those days, and I never felt very confident. I wasn't particularly good or useful, and I was terrified of losing my job, because if I got canned, I'd lose my work visa and I'd have to leave the country. I didn't want to crawl back to Canada in defeat. I tried very hard to blend in—with mixed results. One day I was wearing a blazer with a crest from my parents' yacht club that had a little letter *C* on it. Somebody in a meeting asked if I worked at the Copa at night. I went home and took a razor blade and sliced the crest off.

I didn't have a ton of friends, so on weekends I got the *AIA Guide to Architecture* and would just walk the streets to see what the city looked like up close. I discovered that it's not this huge mass of stone and commerce you imagine from afar; it's an exquisite mosaic of neighborhoods and people and families and schools. Because it was the area north of the Prince George, I had, and still have, a great appreciation for Murray Hill. I think it's the most unchanged part of New York. It's never really been discovered in the Dumbo or Williamsburg sense, but it has never been forgotten either. And in those days it was filled with stewardesses.

GARY
SHTEYNGART

{ writer }
arrived: 1979

Coming to America in the late 1970s after a child-hood spent in the Soviet Union was equivalent to stumbling off a monochromatic cliff and landing in pure Technicolor. I remember myself, as an intensely curious child, pressing my nose to the window of the taxiing jetliner, watching the first hints of America passing by. The sweep of what used to be JFK's Pan

Am terminal with its "flying saucer" roof that told us we had left one century and landed in another; the purposeful, swift, but oddly humane stride of the first Americans brushing past us at immigration; the odd expanse of the springtime sky that didn't press down on Queens, as the Russian sky had trampled my stretch of Leningrad, but flowed past in waves, allotting a bit of itself to each red-bricked or aluminum-sided house, and to each of the lucky families that dwelled within.

The science fiction aspect, the intensity of arrival, did not leave me for the next hours, weeks, months. I felt like the convert to a new religion: everything was revelation. I will never forget the ride from the airport, my first highway overpass, the way the car (a private car, no less, bigger than three Soviet Ladas) leaned into the curve hundreds of feet above the greenery of Queens. Here we were floating through air as surely as the passengers of the airplane that had delivered us. And buckled into the back seat, with my parents also leaning into the airborne curve, I felt the same emotions I would experience when choking upon my first cheesy American pizza slice years later—elation, visceral excitement, but also fear. How would I ever measure up to the gentle, smiling giants strolling this land who launched their cars like cosmonauts into the infinite American sky and who lived like lords in their little castles on forty-by-one-hundred-foot lots in Kew Gardens, Queens? How would I ever learn to speak English the way they did, in a way so informal and direct, but with the words circling the air like homing pigeons, the ease of their landing in one's ear, the instinctive way in which they knew how to find home?

But we found home too. The two unlikely words that I would learn in my new English: *garden apartment*. Our first place was modest by local standards, but it fronted a beautiful patch of trees and grass, where the squirrels soon became my new friends. I shared with these squirrels many American peanuts, those salty, double-barreled sources of endless nutrition, and together we shed our native furs to welcome summer in New York, our bodies sweaty, happy, strumming with possibility. The Americans my family met were kinder than we had expected, kinder than any human beings we had known, and they furnished us with little gifts they thought Russians would like, for example cigarettes (though my parents didn't smoke) and little toy cars (as far as I was concerned, they made all other gifts redundant). I remember lying on the grass, my loyal squirrels chirping in the trees above me, as I zipped a Hot Wheels Chevrolet Impala off a glossy pack of Marlboros. Those memories *are* my New World, because even to a child who knows little, some parts of the planet are instinctively, intrinsically, more welcoming than others. And in the garden apartment above, I see my mother watching me from the window, the woman who had abandoned her own dying mother in Leningrad to bring me to America.

DANNY MEYER

{ restaurateur }

arrived: 1980

The first night I moved to New York was the night that John Lennon was shot. I had gotten burned out working for a political campaign in Chicago, and had decided to try New York for a year to get it out of my system. So I slept on the floor of some college friends' apartment, and that weekend I went to Central Park for the Lennon vigil. It was an amazing feeling: a moment of community and realizing that this horrible tragedy had brought that many human beings together. I wasn't as much scared by the violent act as attracted to the beauty of its aftermath.

I ended up taking a $16,000-a-year job selling electronic tags designed to stop shoplifters, and soon after that I became the top salesman in the company. I drove a powder-blue Volkswagen Rabbit to every corner of New York. I had the Duane Reade and Burlington Coat Factory Warehouse accounts. I owned the fur district. I got to know every Sephardic Jewish family who owned mom-and-pop drugstores in Brooklyn and Queens.

I lived in a walk-up railroad apartment on Seventy-ninth and First. I remember cooking out of a hibachi grill on the fire escape, and waking up to the smell of the doughnuts from the shop below us. I ate the best rotisserie chicken in the world from a deli called Eddie's, and bought link sausages and sauerkraut from Germantown on Eighty-sixth Street. A block and a half away were David's Cookies, and I had never had chocolate-chip cookies like that in my life.

I had started taking cooking classes partly as a way to meet girls, but when I got to my first class, I found that everyone was in their fifties. I entertained all the time, hosting lovely brunches where I would go out and source the best cheeses and pâtés I could find, which was a big deal for a twenty-two-year-old back then. One day I saw two guys wheeling an espresso maker down the street. They were opening a twenty-eight-seat joint called Trastevere, which would soon get three stars from the *Times*. I got to know the restaurant business through them, and I subscribed to Seymour Britchky and Andy Birsch's restaurant newsletters. I became the go-to person among my friends for anyone who wanted to know where to eat.

When the company wanted me to move to London, I quit and took the Kaplan LSAT course. On the eve of taking the test, I went out to Elio's on Second Avenue with my aunt and uncle. I'm saying I don't want to be a lawyer, and my uncle responds, "All I've ever heard you talk about since you were a kid is food and restaurants. Why don't you just go into the restaurant business?" No one talked about going into the restaurant business back then—not unless you were from Greece or Italy or Czechoslovakia. So I took the LSATs anyway, but my next call was to my college buddy, asking if he would take a restaurant-management class with me. Three classes in, my buddy dropped out. But he felt so bad, he arranged an interview for me with Eugene Fracchia, the owner of Pesca, who looked me up and down and gave me the job of assistant manager on the spot. Two hundred and fifty dollars a week. And it turned out I loved it.

SUSANNE BARTSCH

{ party promoter
arrived: 1981 }

I came to New York for love. Doesn't everybody? I never planned to live here. I came on Valentine's Day for a little affair with a man who asked me to visit him in his apartment at the Chelsea Hotel. It was all fabulously romantic—until, of course, he fell in love with someone else. But I fell in love with New York. And I kept the apartment.

Oh wait, no—I first came for the opening of Studio 54. But the romance story is the story we tell ourselves. I had been in London having every kind of fun in the rock scene there. I was very close with Mick Jagger and Jimmy Page and the New Romantic crowd. But London was starting to be over—there was so much that was inspiring that it got exhausting—and I was feeling like somewhat of a creature of habit. Whereas in New York there was nothing. You could put a flower in your hair and people thought it was fashion. You could make the nothing into whatever you wanted; New York was like a bare platform begging for set dressings.

I opened a little shop on Thompson Street, back when nobody was in SoHo. I made a New London in New York. I went to street fashion and the schools, not the established designers. I found Marc Jacobs at Parsons doing this wonderful knitwear, and I scooped up all this fun, Gaudí-esque jewelry by people like Robert Lee Morris. Donna Karan would come into my shop—for inspiration, probably, but who knows?

There was a culture mob and a few underground

clubs at the time, but it was very blah. Guys would take off their shirts and dance-dance-dance, but it was not about having "The Look." So I started wearing my Stephen Jones and just showing off.

In 1986, Savage opened as a secretary's after-hours club on West Twenty-third Street. But it really became something when I started hosting the party on Tuesdays, and I have to say, that's when it all started. You couldn't just show up and say "I'm here," like it was Studio 54. You had to have something happening—some drama. People started wearing head-to-toe looks. It was feathers and sequins and platform shoes and leggings and glitter. There was a guy named Stewart who made all my wigs, including my favorite big-haired purple-and-black wig, which I called Babe.

But it wasn't just Savage, of course. Arthur Weinstein had a club called the Continental on Twenty-fifth Street that was a little nothing apartment that, one night a week, he turned into something special. People would go to the Jefferson on Fourteenth Street, or the Palladium, Danceteria, Area, MK, Club 57—and then Disco Donuts afterwards. You started seeing people doing lots of shots. It was part of the pace: Slippery

Nipples, B-52s, Mudslides, Jägermeister—all washed down with Rolling Rock and Absolut.

The clubs became gardens for wonderful, special, fantastic, genius orphans of the mainstream. It was a kid culture: enthusiastic and unguarded, where things like the drag taboo became as acceptable—as required, really—as champagne. And it was so necessary and urgent. That's the thing. The city had been in financial ruin, cocaine and freebasing were ruining everyone's lives, and AIDS was destroying all the fun people. I remember going to see Klaus Nomi in the hospital and we had to wear masks because nobody knew what AIDS was. I remember the cops in the East Village wouldn't say "Don't do drugs," because they knew they had lost that battle; they would say, "Don't do these certain drugs with these certain pictures on the packaging." But this was when we needed to have fun the most.

I came to learn that New York is very appreciative. Yes, I know it is ultimately a city of PR—that they tell you what you want to hear and make you think you need what you do not really need. I know there's always a million-dollar deal in the works on Monday that has fallen through by Friday. But there is always the next Monday. London was all jigsaw jungles and roundabouts and confusion. New York's geography is direct and enabling; it helps people meet and get things done. It's very hard to get lost. And in fact, it's very easy to find yourself.

COLUM McCANN

{ writer
arrived: 1982 }

Drunk and sober, high and low, off and on, up and down, lost and found, New York has been my city for fifteen years now. It's a vast mystery to me, like it is to most New Yorkers, how this ugly lovely town became *my* lovely ugly town, this gorgeous rubbish heap of a place, this city of the timeless Now, with little of the style of Paris, little of the beauty of Rome, little of the history of London, and not even much of the dear dirty dereliction of my hometown, Dublin.

New York is a fiction of sorts, a construct, a story, into which you can walk at any moment and at any angle, and end up blindsided, turned upside down, changed.

There are dozens of moments I can recall from the early days when I first got to the city as a naive young Dubliner. I was seventeen years old and visiting for the summer. I ran the Midtown streets as a gopher for Universal Press Syndicate. I rushed for sandwiches, answered phones, delivered parcels. My ears popped in the Time-Life elevators. On a July afternoon I lay down in the middle of the Avenue of the Americas and looked up at the skyscrapers. I laughed as people stepped over and around me. Later I sat in the back of the Lion's Head pub and dreamed myself into writing days. I bluffed my way into Limelight. On the D train I nursed a cocaine itch back to Brighton Beach, where I rented a cockroached room. It was all a fantastic fever dream: even now the moments collide into each other and my memory is decorated by a series of mirrors flashing light into chambers of sound and color, graffiti and roar. I left it after a few months, back to Dublin, enchanted and dazzled.

But I truly fell in love with the city many years later, in the early 1990s, on my second stint, when I wasn't quite sure if I was meant to be here at all, and it was a quiet moment that did it for me, one of those little glancing shoulder-rubs that New York can deal out at any time of the day, in any season, in any weather, in any place—even on the fiercely unfashionable Upper East Side.

It had snowed in the city. Two feet of it over the course of the night. It was the sort of snow that made the city temporarily magical, before all the horn-blowing and slush puddles and piles of dog crap crowning the melt.

A very thin little path had been cleared on Eighty-second Street between Lexington and Third, just wide enough for two able-bodied people to squeeze through. The snow was piled high on either side. A small canyon, really, in the middle of the footpath. On the street—a quiet street at the best of times, if anything can be quiet in New York—the cars were buried under drifts. The telegraph wires sagged. The underside of the tree branches appeared like brush-strokes on the air. Nothing moved. The brownstones looked small against so much white. In the distance sounded a siren, but that was all, making the silence more complete.

I saw her from a distance halfway down the block. She was already bent into the day. She wore a head-scarf. Her coat was old enough to have once been fashionable. She was pushing along a silver frame. Her walk was crude, slow, laborious. With her frame, she took the whole width of the alley. There was no space to pass her.

There is always a part of New York that must keep moving—as if breath itself depends on being frantic, hectic, overwhelmed. I thought to myself that I should just clamber over the snowbank and walk down the other side of the street. But I waited and watched. Snow still fell on the shoveled walkway. Her silver frame slipped and slid. She looked up, caught my eye, gazed down again. There was the quality of the im-migrant about her: something dutiful, sad, brave. A certain *saudade*, a longing for another place.

As she got closer, I noticed her gloves were beau-tifully stenciled with little jewels. Her headscarf was pulled tight around her lined face. She shoved the silver frame over a small ridge of ice, walked the final few feet, and stopped in front of me.

The silence of strangers.

But then she leaned forward and said in a whisper: "Shall we dance?"

She took off one glove and reached her hand out, and with the silver frame between us, we met on the pavement. Then she let go of my hand. I bent to one knee and bowed slightly to her. She grinned and put her glove back on, said nothing more, took a hold of her silver frame, and moved on, a little quicker now, along the corridor of snow and around the corner.

I knew nothing of her, nothing at all, and yet she had made the day unforgettable.

She was my New York.

Still is.

DAVID RAKOFF

{ writer
arrived: 1982 }

M y mother's purse was stolen about an hour before my parents left me in New York to start my freshman year of college. She noticed it missing from the
back of her café chair just as we were finishing up
our lunch at an outdoor table at a long-disappeared
Italian place at 111th and Broadway. The handbag
had probably been gone for a while, but like cartoon

characters who wander off of cliffs but only fall once they realize they have done so, I felt the solid ground disappear from under my feet and my life in New York begin.

Truthfully, I found the theft thrilling, even as it sharpened whatever anxiety my folks must have been feeling. The robbery conferred a modicum of street cred with zero injury, and I needed all the help I could get. I was a sophisticated sissy, having grown up near the center of Toronto, a cosmopolitan city of three million people. But displaying cultural literacy and knowing the difference between shit and Shinola are two distinctly separate realms. Being able to quote entire scenes of *The Philadelphia Story* from memory or paint a good facsimile of Van Gogh's *Sunflowers* (Large. On my dorm room wall) won't do you a bit of good in the real world. At seventeen, I knew nothing, and I looked it. A whelp of barely five and a half feet, I was markedly shorter and less developed than the boys I saw unloading boxes and suitcases. Compared to most of them, I was a tentatively pubescent cherub, encased in puppy fat with a face open to experience that seemed to beg: *Please hurt me.*

I looked at the purse-snatching as an early and

painless inoculation from violence, no small matter in the city back when the prospect was still real
enough. New York in 1982 was only beginning to
shake off the traces of its "Ford to City: Drop Dead"
near bankruptcy. Infrastructure was still crumbling,
the subways were still covered in graffiti. The term
yuppie would not be commonplace for another few
years (and it would be at least that amount of time
before the city opened its first Banana Republic or
Cajun restaurant to clothe and feed them). Coffee
still meant a paper cupful from Chock Full o'Nuts.
There was a remaining franchise at 116th Street and
Broadway, probably unchanged since 1961, still boast-
ing its undulating lunch counter in buttercream For-
mica, while one block down, a warning shot across the
caffeinated bow of the neighborhood, was a doomed
black-lacquer establishment with the almost parodi-
cally striving name Crepes and Cappuccino. The own-
ers had wrapped the sickly tree out front in bright blue
fairy lights, which only illuminated the empty interior
in a dejected glow. It lasted less than a year. The colos-
sus towering over this particular moment shuddering
between decadence and recovery was not Bartholdi's
Lady Liberty, but the first of Calvin Klein's bronzed

gods, high above Times Square. Leaning back, eyes closed, in his blinding white underpants against a sinuous form in similarly white Aegean plaster, his gargantuan, sleeping, groinful beauty was simultaneously Olympian and intimate, awesome and comforting. Here was the city in briefs: uncaring, cruelly beautiful, and out of reach.

Not all of New York's loveliness was stratospheric and unattainable, but at street level it was mixed in with the threat of harm, which was ever present, if in a somewhat exaggerated and highly prized form. We had been warned that the neighborhood around the university could turn dodgy in a matter of footsteps, but it was a matter of pride to have dipped one's toe into its scary waters. Morningside Park, for example: not since the age of medieval maps—wherein the world simply ends, beyond which all is monster-filled roil—has a region been so terrifyingly uncharted and freighted with peril as Morningside Park in the early 1980s. To venture in was to die, plain and simple. There were other terrifying rumors abounding, like the one about the boy in the hideous Gwathmey Siegel designed dormitory who narrowly avoided the bullet that came through his window and lodged itself in the plaster above his head. The shot had come from—where else?—Morningside Park. Another boy, walking back to his room on upper Broadway one drizzling evening, had had his wallet demanded. He handed it over, and for his compliance had his teeth knocked out with the hard metal barrel of a gun. The boy-who-was-pistol-whipped-in-the-rain grabbed us with all the cheap poetry and tamped bathos of a Tom Waits song. It was doubly satisfying to me, since whenever he came up in conversation, I could say, "Tell me about it. I was robbed my first day here."

Mere days into the school year, my floor counselor, an elder statesman in his senior year, knocked on my door and gave me a stapled Xerox of the Joan Didion essay "Goodbye to All That." The flattery of being singled out for such a gift is what made me read it immediately, with little comprehension. "All I could do during those [first] three days was talk long-distance to the boy I already knew I would never marry in the spring. I would stay in New York, I told him, just six months, and I could see the Brooklyn Bridge from my window. As it turned out the bridge was the Triborough, and I stayed eight years." I was immune to the humor or irony in this passage. What I took away from it was the hope—as unlikely as sprouting wings, it seemed to me back then—that I might one day be as old as twenty, or have logged eight years here, to acquire that youth-viewed-at-a-distance weariness, to be able to rattle off the names of the city's lesser-known bridges.

It was what I took away from most every encounter: an almost obliterating desire to "pass" as a New Yorker, to authentically resemble one of the denizens of the movie *Manhattan*. More than the Deco penthouse aeries of characters in old musicals, more than the moral elasticity and heartless grit of backstage Broadway in *All That Jazz*, perhaps on par with the gin-swilling savagery of *All About Eve*, it was the city as embodied in *Manhattan* I ached for. The high-strung friends with terrible problems, the casual infidelities, the rarefied bohemianism—ERA fund-raisers in the garden at MoMA, gallery-hopping followed by filling one's simple grocery list at Dean & DeLuca.

There was no one specific moment when the rigorous self-consciousness gave way to authenticity. It was more of a dim realization that the very act of playing the "Are we a New Yorker yet?" game means you aren't one yet. But it eventually happens, dawning on you after the fact, tapping you on the shoulder after you've passed it. It comes from an accretion of shitty jobs, deeply felt friendships that last, deeply felt friendships that end, funerals, marriages, divorces, births, and betrayals, and you wake up one day to realize that you passed the eight-year mark decades prior; that you are older than all of the characters in *Manhattan*, with the possible exception of Bella Abzug; that you have been to a party in the garden at MoMA and watched the sun come up over Sutton Place and the Fifty-ninth Street Bridge and decided that, in the end, you'd rather stay home; that only a rich moron would buy his groceries at Dean & DeLuca; and that, as fun and Margo Channing as it might seem to be drunk and witty and cutting, it's probably better in the long run to be kind. These are all realizations endemic to aging anywhere, I am sure. It must happen in other cities, but I've really only ever been a grown-up here.

As for my mother's pocketbook, it was found later that evening, emptied of valuables and abandoned in a building lobby in Morningside Heights. Some good

Samaritan had gone through her phone book and found the number of a New York friend, who eventually tracked me down in my dorm room. It made the city seem like a shtetl, a fact that after the better part of three decades I realize is more true than not.

HAROLD
EVANS

{ journalist
arrived: 1983 }

Tina Brown and I couldn't have gotten off the boat
any more unaware of New York life. The year before,
we had gotten married in Ben Brantley's garden in
East Hampton, and we had spent one night in the Algonquin. We saw Lena Horne, and had dinner with
Lauren Bacall, which was very exciting. But then Tina
had to return to *Tatler* in London, and I left a couple

days later. We had visited New York many times, of course, but we were not prepared to live here, and had no idea of the subterranean current of New York life.

Our first apartment was a disaster: a sublet on Third Avenue for which we paid rent by putting dollar bills in a hat. I'm supposed to be an investigative journalist, but I was too concerned about getting the apartment and so decided this was perfectly normal. We were instructed to speak to the doorman with assumed names. One day I opened a cupboard and out fell tons of pornography. I shouldn't have been looking in the cupboard—it wasn't my apartment. If I hadn't been about to teach a college class on ethics, I might have questioned the ethics of it all.

When we realized we would like to be treated like law-abiding citizens, Tina got us an apartment on Central Park South. Another disaster. This one had cockroaches, and since we were close to the ground floor, I hesitated to go anywhere near the window in my pajamas. And living on Central Park South is like being a part of a parade.

We moved again to a two-bedroom at 300 East Fifty-sixth, where one of the rooms had a bed that disappeared into the wall, and if you weren't careful you'd disappear with the bed. We soon realized that New Yorkers don't muck up their kitchens by doing breakfast. Instead I would go to the Palace restaurant off Lex. We got in the habit of walking down Second Avenue and trying every restaurant on the left-hand side, which is very interesting because you go from the tolerable to the absolutely marvelous to the intolerable in the space of six blocks. A space was good or reasonable, or it was full of shouting maniacs. Mimi's I liked very much, and the places populated by Irishmen were jolly. We couldn't entertain many people at the apartment, so we'd usually take people out to Mortimer's.

Within a very short time, the New York vortex kicked in. When you're on the outer edges you can swim quite happily in cool waters, but as you get closer and get to know more people, you get sucked into a level of activity that is calculated to drive you crazy. It was very exciting—and very 1980s. People arrived in stretch limos. At the same time, I was astounded by the drug transactions I'd see on street corners, even in white-collar Midtown, outside the New York Public Library. It was grim as hell, and all this alongside the intellectual excitement of media life and America being on top of the world. It was like going to dinner with some wonderful person and looking underneath the table and finding mice droppings.

KEITH HERNANDEZ

{ baseball player

arrived: 1983 }

New York was the last place I wanted to be, down there with Cleveland, Oakland, and Detroit. I was a guy from San Francisco, and I had already made something of myself, winning the World Series with the Cardinals, so it's not like I was some kid getting off at the bus station in Midtown all full of wonder. And nobody wants to be traded midseason.

But I joined the Mets in June 1983. At first I was put up in a hotel at LaGuardia, which was a terrible existence. I eventually moved to Greenwich until I got divorced. Then Rusty Staub, a New York fixture, told me, "Look, man, if you're going to be single, don't live in Connecticut. It's all in the city."

So I rented a place for a year until Fred Wilpon, the Mets owner who was also a real-estate guy, offered to sell me a condo at Forty-ninth and Second. It had been decorated by some interior decorator in Chicago, and they put all my clothes and luggage in a pile ten feet high—no lie—in the middle of the living room. Ed Lynch, a starting pitcher, was crashing with me while his condo was being finished. I went out one day, and when I came back he had unpacked all my stuff. I got his dinners for a month after that.

We'd go downtown. SoHo was this pocket of the city where you could just get out of a cab, wander around, and have a great night no matter what. And I really got into the restaurants. You know, you could do a ball game and then still have dinner after. At eleven! That doesn't happen in the Midwest. Fanelli's, Palladium, Chin Chin, Smith & Wollensky, Lutèce . . . And you'd be a fool to live here and not take advantage of the cultural stuff. So I would go to Broadway plays and even some operas. I met Plácido Domingo backstage once. The guy is a huge baseball fan, and he said "Sorry, I have a cold, I sang like a .230 hitter. Next time, I promise I'll be a .300 singer for you."

Back then, of course, the Mets were terrible, so I would be incognito. As we got better, I would go out, and it would be all or nothing. Nobody would recognize me, or they all would. And, man, for about six weeks after we won the '86 World Series, I couldn't pay for dinner anywhere in the city. People would, I kid you not, send over bottles and bottles of free Cristal. Ridiculous. It's one thing to become a New Yorker; it's so much weirder to become a New Yorker that all the other New Yorkers know.

IRA GLASS

{ radio host
arrived: 1984 }

I first moved here when the woman I was with decided to go to NYU law school. We lived in married-
student housing, though we weren't married, and they
were really just dorms. We were assigned a freshman
dorm, and I was twenty-five and had never felt older in
my life. We split up after a few months.

We had moved from Washington, and I was trying

to learn to write radio stories. I wasn't a terribly fast study, so I did other things, like working as a temp secretary. I made about fifteen thousand dollars a year. I remember walking by the Dallas Barbecue on the northeast side of Washington Square Park. I would look at people eating in the restaurant and think to myself, Someday I'll be able to afford to eat in a place like that.

After the NYU dorms, I lived in a series of cheap apartments, the worst of which was at Rivington and Allen. That was a truly dangerous neighborhood. I would get out of the subway on Houston Street at night, and there'd be drug dealers and prostitutes and crack vials on the streets, and I always had to make the decision, Should I run? And I thought, well, that's just going to look so uncool. But often I would run.

I rented an illegal sublet that cost me $145 a month; if anyone questioned what I was doing there, I was under strict instructions to say I was visiting somebody. The apartment had a smell to it that came up through the floorboards. My roommate had come to New York to do art but then had gotten into a dispute with the landlord, and literally, the dispute with the landlord took up every ounce of brainpower that

she had. She was suing him for stuff that got dam-
aged when the roof had caved in, and she was forever
going on and on about the proceedings and how un-
fair he was and how he did one lousy thing to her or
another. She became unable to do anything but think
about this apartment. She was like a character out of
a Tom Wolfe novel—her life had made her crazy—
and that just seemed to sum up so exactly something
about this city.

PARKER POSEY

{ actress
arrived: 1984 }

I was sixteen the first time I came to New York City. I had two close girlfriends who had grown up in Manhattan that I met at the University of North Carolina School of the Arts, Tanya and Sasha. We had taken the acting program there and I visited them the following spring. My parents and I arrived from a small town in the Deep South into the city and in the cab as

I sensed their fear of the unknown, I could sense my attraction to it. I looked into all the cars passing us, amazed that it could all exist without people crashing into each other—what instinct, I thought! Where does it come from? It all seemed cheoreographed to me, and unbelievable. I thought: this is a place to truly put your trust in God, to test accidental nature, to live like an Existentialist!

Tanya and Sasha and I sang and danced through the streets, jumping on park benches, swinging on lamp posts, doing silly dances and no one judged us or seemed to even notice. People and their lives would walk by and I loved the fleetingness of it all, loved that they dressed like they didn't care. Some people looked as though they'd been in the same clothes all week and I thought: yeah, who cares! I loved asking for directions and talking to strangers I would never see again. I almost got run over by a bike messenger, something I had never seen in my life. It felt like a miracle I wasn't dead.

Sasha's mom, a painter, lived in a loft in SoHo, which seemed to me like a huge attic but without the furniture. A bed was somewhere behind huge paintings that leaned against each other like giant books in the middle of the living room—which was the whole apartment, the whole house! Exposed brick and wooden floors, exposed light bulbs, a homemade bathroom with a tub on a platform of mosaic tiles, and her mother's jewelry all around—earrings from Afghanistan and other exotic things that looked like travel to faraway places. I thought about her neighbors just on the other side of the wall, and I got a glass and pressed the bottom to my ear and tried to hear them. Endless entertainment. I couldn't wait to live like this.

We climbed the fire escape to smoke cigarettes and take pictures of ourselves in the sunset looking serious. And we played ping-pong and pool somewhere in the West Village and drank beer and ate burgers at the Corner Bistro. Sasha liked The Clash and I liked The Jam, and the Beastie Boys were just beginning. A cute guy offered to buy the jeans I was wearing for a hundred dollars and I almost took him up on it but then I thought, what would I wear? He said they were for his girlfriend. Now I think he was hitting on me.

NAOMI
CAMPBELL

{ model
arrived: 1986 }

At sixteen years old, I was summoned by Anna Wintour to work for American *Vogue* on a Steven Meisel shoot, and I was put on the British Airways Concorde. As we were leaving the airport I told the driver, "I want to go on the Graffiti Train." I had seen *The Warriors*. All I'd ever seen of New York was the movies.

Christy Turlington and I were roommates in a loft

on Centre Street, in the same building where the fashion photographer Arthur Elgort had his studio. I've always attributed my success to Christy, because of how supportive she was when people wouldn't book models of color for their shows.

My first summer in New York was tough. I didn't mind the heat, but everybody had left the city and I felt a bit lonely. I hadn't yet learned the seasons. I fell in love with Central Park, though. I'd go to a delicatessen and stock up for a picnic with friends. I'd visit the boat houses and watch people playing music and beating drums. Nell's had just opened on West Fourteenth Street. Prince used to go there a lot. But I liked it because it was cozy, and I always stayed with my friends.

I would go to see the House of Extravaganza, dance at clubs, or hang out on the West Side Highway, near where I used to shoot. One time I saw one of the voguers get knocked down on the highway, and I remember a private ambulance refused to take him. That was a little shocking; I didn't understand the idea of medical insurance, as opposed to the way emergency service worked in England. I remember calling home and saying, "Mom, guess what I saw today." And she was like, "Get your medical insurance."

AUDRA McDONALD

{ actress
arrived: 1988 }

I had just turned eighteen, and I was getting ready to attend Juilliard. I came here with $300 and was living at the Narragansett, a residential hotel on Ninety-third and Broadway. Now, Ninety-third and Broadway in 1988 was a very interesting place to be. There were certain hours at the Narragansett that you just didn't ride the elevator, because you wanted to live. That whole *Friends* thing with the naked guy across the way? We had one of those right across from us who would watch us and masturbate. A lot of the people in that building were drug addicts, but they took care of the Juilliard students, too. They were like, *No, no, no, don't go to that bodega. No, no, no, I'll go get it.*

MIKE MYERS

{ comedian arrived: 1988 }

I was from Toronto and had this fantasy that the only time I would ever come to New York would be if I had an audition for *Saturday Night Live*. That was a very exclusive condition. But in fact, that is what happened: I was called to meet Lorne Michaels, the producer of *Saturday Night Live*. It was one of those magical moments—not just because I saw how beautiful and vibrant the city was, but also because my superstitious belief that I should never come for another reason had paid off. I landed at LaGuardia, and the cabbie took the Fifty-ninth Street Bridge, which I now know to be a strange choice. (Why not the Triborough?) I looked up at the city as we crossed the river, and it brought me to tears.

By the time I got to *SNL*, it was very family oriented. The cast was all married, and many of them with kids. It was a lot of "Do you want to go jogging with me in the park?" and "I'll meet you at the Imagine Circle!" But I quickly fell in love with Central Park, and the decorative elements of the Upper West Side brownstones, and, even though it's Helvetica, the fonts in the subway system.

Dana Carvey told me that everyone lived on the Upper West Side. One day I was walking down Amsterdam, and people saw me and waved. I had that horrible feeling of, *I don't remember these people.* So I came up and said, "Hey!" They were shocked that I said hello to them. They said, "You're the new dude on *Saturday Night Live!*" And I was like, *Oh my God—I'm a famous person now!*

CHLOË SEVIGNY

{ actress
arrived: 1991 }

I grew up in Connecticut and went to the city with my family for big holidays. But I started going on my own when I was a freshman in high school, skipping school and staying overnight on the weekends. We'd hang out in Washington Square Park with all the skater kids and punkers and pot dealers. The north part of the park was the skater side (because there's a slope the kids would skate down to get speed), and the south side was more hip-hop. By the time I was a junior, I think my parents were a little nervous. Sometimes I'd lie and say I was at a friend's house in Greenwich. They would not have been happy if they knew that I was at a rave all night long and then sleeping in the park. But not like a homeless person—like a teenager. I was with a group of cute kids.

My sophomore year, I saw the Sugarcubes at Roseland. Björk was friends with all of the club kids, and at the end of the show they all came onstage. Now, this is before I knew what club kids were, and I was shocked by the sight of them all on the stage with her. They looked like complete freaks. I later became friends with some of them. A lot of them didn't like me, though—usually because the gay boys that they liked, liked me. It didn't help that I looked like a boy then, with my shaved head.

I read Luc Sante's *Low Life* and discovered the Lower East Side. Tompkins Square Park we never went to—it was gnarly. I remember going to Avenue A and being really scared. I was young and from Connecticut:

it just felt like a situation I didn't want to put myself in. But Washington Square Park was very safe. Some of the kids thought I was just a freaky girl who stared a lot. And it's true, I was staring at everybody. I was just fascinated by these kids.

AMY SEDARIS

{ comedienne
arrived: 1993 }

The first thing I saw when I came to New York was a man leaning up against a wall, shitting. Perfect! My brother David had taken me to Chinatown to see a chicken dance, and it was immediately clear that New York was just much more stimulating than Chicago. I was never scared in Chicago. Here your fear was sitting right in front of you. But I loved it. David and I lived with our friend Paul Dinello in a gigantic loft on Chambers Street. It was a strange area, with no grocery stores or anything around. The loft was $1,500, fifteen hundred square feet, and really cold. I remember brewing tea and throwing the tea bags into our spare room, just to watch them freeze.

I started waitressing at Marion's, and then got a job at Gourmet Garage. After work David and I would go to Balducci's and look at their prepared food and then go home and try to make what we saw. We shopped at Western Beef all the time. Waitressing was always fun. I like to wait on people, I like to work around food, I like to make cash, and I like to hear people complain.

RUFUS WAINWRIGHT

{ musician
arrived: 1994 }

My New York life didn't really begin until 1999, but I first moved here in 1994, after I'd fallen in love with a heroin addict in Montreal. I was still smarting from that failed relationship and had to get out of the vicinity of my dark love. So I came to New York and worked three jobs: at Film Forum; at the Lion's Head, on Sheridan Square; and as the houseboy for a Broadway producing family who lived on Park Avenue. I would also perform here and there, mostly at an old jazz club called Deanna's in the East Village, but I couldn't make enough money or any friends. Nobody was interested in my point of view. I tried to perform at the Lower East Side club Sin-é, but they refused my tape three times. I'd go to the old Crowbar to see Misstress Formika, during the East Village Renaissance that I had absolutely nothing to do with.

So I moved back to Montreal and started doing a lot of shows there. I was signed to DreamWorks Records and made my first album while living in L.A. When I came back to New York in '97, DreamWorks got me a gig at Fez, which was a bit of a nightmare. I opened for a folksinger named Jonatha Brooke, who is very nice but whose fans are assholes. I think they would purposely speak louder when I was onstage. One time, a bunch of people came in on Rollerblades and sat in front of me really drunk while I was trying to sing about dying opera divas.

I ended up hanging out a lot with this girl Lisa, a really party-hearty hard-core *Sex and the City* person. Lisa was in advertising, and her crowd wasn't necessarily an artistic mélange. We'd go to the Wax Bar in

SoHo, and I was their gay-artist mascot. But one night I saw Kiki & Herb do their Christmas show at P.S. 122. It was earth-shattering; it gave me a focal point of where I wanted to go.

I went back to L.A. to write my second album, *Poses*. L.A. was also where I learned how to drink and do drugs, how to scope out the dealer and get into the party, and how to drive drunk (which I don't do anymore). So when I finally returned to New York, in the summer of 1999, I was like a heat-seeking missile to find out what was happening, where was the fun, where were the goods, and who I wanted to go home with. I had very long hair and wore Greek caftans and posed as a romantic, almost Pre-Raphaelite androgynous person. I moved into a closet-size $1,800 apartment in the Chelsea Hotel because my friend Lorca Cohen told me her father Leonard used to live there, and that I should too. I met this guy Walt Paper, who brought me into the remnants of that club-kid world, which had just collapsed. We met the drag performer Lily of the Valley and a fashion designer named Zaldy, and the four of us became a quartet who were at every party and in every hot tub and on every beach.

We went to the Boiler Room and Beige and the

Cock, where Miss Guy would DJ this eclectic mix of rock and roll, Nirvana, and Dolly Parton. I drank a lot, starting around noon and going on till four in the morning. I was so blissfully ignorant of any kind of danger or defeat. I was so confident that I was brilliant and indestructible and could drink and sleep with people as much as I wanted. I no longer have that magic blankness. But when I think back on it, I'm proud of having cracked the code of living life to the fullest, and that it didn't take me down—though it very nearly did in the end.

MAGGIE GYLLENHAAL

{ actress
arrived: 1995 }

I grew up in L.A. and moved back here to go to college at Columbia, where I lived in the dorm for the first two years. I had a boyfriend who lived on Ludlow Street, and I couldn't believe a place as alive and wild as that existed. I wanted to drop out of school and hang out there. I remember there was this guy who would take PCP. And when he did, everyone on the block would stop what they were doing and lock the doors and hide from him as he smashed car windows. My boyfriend had a teeny-tiny apartment that he shared with another guy. They had built bunk beds. And I would sleep over. The roommate would still be there, but we figured it out, like you do when you're that age. We would use the Pink Pony like it was our kitchen and living room. I felt it was such a great way to live. I don't know how I'd manage that now.

MICHAEL LUCAS

{ porn star
arrived: 1997 }

I met a Wall Street guy when I was living in Munich who invited me to move to New York. He was a very difficult person, but he was the only person I knew in the city. We lived on Thirty-ninth Street between Eighth and Ninth, which was depressing. Every day there were these terrible tourists, and every evening it would be even worse, with tranny hustlers and hook-ers. I remember one sad-looking transsexual who had just been punched in the eye. It was all too much.

I had arrived at JFK with a backpack and a little suitcase and $150. I immediately started escorting for $300 an hour and working at the Gaiety Theater. Porn was not my dream; I wanted to be the next Tom Cruise. But I was realistic and practical, and saw my competition in Hollywood, and decided that the opportunity for me was in porn. But it was also depressing, mostly because I was working with straight, rude, gay-for-pay performers. It was a lot of pressure: five shows a day, two performances a show (one clothed, one naked). At first, people didn't want me as their escort because I was not buff enough, or because I had long hair and a thick Russian accent. I said *MUD-un-nuh* instead of *Mah-DAWN-ah*.

After three months, I rented the living room of a DJ from the Gaiety and saved $17,000 to pay six months up front on my own one-bedroom on Barrow Street. The neighborhood felt like a nice suburb of London, and that is when I started to fall in love with New York—even though I just had a mattress on the floor and a rotary phone to call my family. I wore poor-person clothes like Abercrombie & Fitch,

which was very sad, very beige. (You can imagine this.
I was from Germany; I did not know one thing about
style. Eventually, when I started to get some money,
I bought Valentino, because I did not know any better.) I got bad haircuts and shopped in bad supermar-
kets. I learned to cook from marked-down cookbooks
I bought at Barnes & Noble, but I preferred Burger
King. I remember looking in the mirror once in 1997
and not seeing even one ab.

I was poor, but through escorting I was paid to go
out and see rich New York. I was taken to the Metropolitan Opera and *The Lion King* and wonderful Eugene O'Neill plays, to tacky-but-expensive restaurants
like Daniel, and to Upper East Side apartments with
marble bathrooms the size of my apartment. I went
to Beige, the Tuesday-night party at Bowery Bar, and
I realized that you could be stylish.

My biggest obstacle was when clients would pay
with bounced checks or fake addresses. I would call
and demand to be paid, and they would treat me like
I was nothing. It was tough. But I kept the bounced
checks. Ten years later, I Googled the name on one
of them and discovered he is this important man who
sits on many important boards. I called him and de-

manded he pay me three times what he owed me, in cash, or I would make him more famous than I was. He paid me. One should not take advantage of a foreigner. We are tougher than people born here, and we achieve more because we are fighting for it.

ALBERT
HAMMOND
JR.

{ musician
arrived: 1998 }

Getting a job at Kim's Video was harder than join-
ing a band. It was ridiculous: you had to know someone. But I had just moved from L.A., trying to get
away from my friends, who were slow and didn't want
to do anything but get fucked up. I finally met this guy
named Aurelio from the band Calla, and one day he
called and said, "Hey, there's a position for you, do you

want it?" I was like, "I've dropped off *tons* of résumés, now I can just *get* the job?"

It was only a month after living here that I met Julian Casablancas. His father had a modeling agency called Elite, and I walked in one day after recognizing his name on the door. We quickly moved into an apartment on Eighteenth Street. The apartment was shaped like a dumbbell and had a washer and dryer instead of an oven. We each had a bathroom, which was the reason why we got it (he's a mess, I'm neat). When I met Julian, I told him I played guitar. He said, "That's funny, we're looking for a guitar player." When I tried out, I had a fever and didn't play well and thought for sure I didn't get the job. What I didn't know is that he had already decided I would be in the Strokes.

We were really ambitious. It's all Julian and I spoke about every night. We set a goal: we'd be playing shows a year from now. When you first start, it takes you all night just to play through one song and play it right. And we only had rehearsal space in the Music Building in the Garment District on Monday and Wednesday at weird hours, although we'd sneak in at other times, too.

Most nights Julian and I would be at home, and Nikolai, another band member, would come down from uptown, where he worked at a video store. We'd get stoned and watch whatever movie he brought. One time, our fridge was packed so full of Budweiser we took a photo of it. Late at night we'd go to the deli down the street where this guy named Peruvian Love Child would make our salami sandwiches.

We tried everything possible to be friends with bands and play bigger shows with them. We weren't picky. But they were all such dicks—too competitive to get together and make anything. The Mooney Suzuki were megastars to us. We saw them one night at the Cooler in the Meatpacking District. They fucking blew us away. We were just standing there watching how cool they looked onstage. It was beyond amazing.

At first, we didn't go out anywhere cool—just Rudy's, which was near the studio and had free hot dogs and $5 pitchers. But slowly we'd go to bars like Don Hill's and Bar 13 to promote, handing out flyers with stuff from weird 1970s soft-porn movies like *Emmanuelle*. They started to recognize us—"Oh, there's the guys from the Strokes hanging out"—and as a group the five of us were a pretty striking image. We were really cocky. Not in a bad way, we just believed in ourselves and so we were always balls to the wall.

ANDY SAMBERG

{ comedian }
arrived: 1998

I moved to New York with three friends from summer camp. Two of us were going to NYU, and the other two were in that self-loathing, debaucherous postcollege year of self-destruction. We crammed into what probably should have been a two-bedroom apartment on Bleecker and Macdougal and sectioned things off into a four-bedroom by putting up a lot of curtains.

That was an absolute disaster. We were all really broke, and those dudes were out of control. There was no one in the house that did any cleaning, so by halfway through the year there were rats and mice everywhere. I grew up in the Bay Area, so I'm fairly "at one" with nature, but this was different. California nature is lovely. New York nature is disgusting. At first, I was really grossed out by it, but by summertime, I remember lying on my couch watching TV with a water gun, and every time a mouse would run out from behind the TV, I would just spray it. There was no "Let's try and catch them"; it was just like, "Take a hike, buddy."

The mice kind of became a part of the house. We weren't feeding them or anything, but we definitely got less skittish around them. It's interesting how much you can adapt to when you don't have the means to fix it. We did get the sticky traps once. But when one got stuck, we were all too scared to get it and throw it out or kill it. Literally, we were four college-age dudes curled up on the couch listening to it scream for three days. We took turns going back and peeking at it and yelling, "Oh God, it's there! It's dying! It's dying! What do we do?" But you can't get it off; if you pull it, you rip the limbs off. The humane thing to do would have been to smash it with a hammer, but no one had the stomach to do that, so it was pretty awful.

DAVID CHANG

{ chef
arrived: 1999 }

I was teaching English in Japan, right out of college. I had no idea what I wanted to do after that, so I just came to New York because that's where most of my friends were. I stayed with my sister, who was getting her whatever-the-fuck degree at Columbia and lived on Seventy-eighth and First Avenue.

New York was a kick in the ass I was not prepared

for. Of all my friends I knew who moved to New York, only a few still live here; it's a hard mentality, it can consume you, and it can be depressing. A lot of the people I hung around with were stuck in an office, and they hated it, myself included. I worked in a variety of desk jobs as a glorified lackey. It was just drunkenness every night; I'd go anywhere there was an open bar. I remember sitting down and calculating how much money I was spending on alcohol—it was ridiculous.

Eventually I was like, Fuck it, I'm just going to start cooking. I had thought of cooking before, but it was never a reality. Or I didn't think it was a reality. In my parents' eyes, cooking wasn't really a career option; my dad had worked as a dishwasher in New York and had hated it. But food was the only thing I really wanted to do. So I enrolled in cooking school. Everyone thought I was a lunatic.

It was a crazy time to be in school, because there were a lot of people who had cashed out of the dot-com boom and were already millionaires. I got my first restaurant job doing hot apps at Mercer Kitchen after school, and I'd take restaurant reservations at Craft on my days off to make cash. I thought that the staff Tom Colicchio had assembled was one of the best in

New York history, so answering phones was not be-
neath me. I did that for a month and a half, until they
let me work in the kitchen for free. I wound up cutting
vegetables and cleaning mushrooms.

Around that time, Wylie Dufresne had opened 71
Clinton, and it was like an atomic bomb had been det-
onated on New York City. That was the restaurant that
revolutionized food in New York, and people still don't
even realize it. And it transformed the Lower East
Side! I remember being totally surprised and caught
off guard that he had opened a restaurant there, and
in love with the whole idea: a classically trained chef
who had worked with Jean-Georges Vongerichten in
Europe was opening up a restaurant on Clinton Street.
It was so contrarian!

Then I went to Japan and learned about noodles,
and it was just one of those things: I thought, I'm
going to open a noodle bar! It could have been in the
Virginia Beach area or New York; I had more culinary
connections in New York, but I had family connections in Virginia. It just so happened that I saw a lo-
cation that I liked better in New York, and I opened
Momofuku Noodle Bar. I'm glad I chose New York. I
mean, opening a restaurant is impossible, and open-

ing it in New York is the dumbest thing you can do: it's crowded, it's expensive, and all that. But there's just something about New York that I've fallen in love with: it's diverse, you can get any food you want, it's condensed, and there's a certain camaraderie. Every city I go to, I compare to New York.

MICHEL
GONDRY

{ filmmaker
arrived: 2002 }

M̲y first impression was that it was impossible to
sleep in New York. I had moved here a few months
after 9/11, as the city was waking up from its trauma.
We were preparing to shoot *Eternal Sunshine of the Spot-
less Mind*. I stayed for two months at the Gramercy
Hotel, but I didn't like that area very much. You don't
have the feeling that the pressure goes down at night.

I moved seven times in the next five years, looking for places where it gets absolutely quiet at night.

The film was paying for me, so they sent me to ridiculously expensive places on the Golden Coast: those blocks between Fifth and Sixth avenues and Ninth and Tenth streets. The super of one of them was a sick, crazy person. If I had a guest coming, she wanted to charge me for using more water. She sacked us because my son was a little too noisy for her taste, and I had sweet thoughts of cold revenge for her. I wanted to pour a pot of red paint on the mat at the entrance—something really sticky that takes days to dry—so people would walk through it and spread the red paint everywhere. I didn't do it because I knew I would be caught immediately, but it made me feel good when I tried to fall asleep at night.

I started to appreciate how in New York, as opposed to Paris, you can have an idea in the morning and make it happen in the afternoon. And how if you're waiting in a line, you can start a conversation with people you don't know. In France, you look a little deranged if you do that. As I started to make friends, I used to go to this bar called Lit in the East Village, which I liked because it felt like old punk rock—dusty and not trendy at all. But soon my son came to live with me. He was very independent. We'd go bicycling, and he would take me to places where he had done graffiti tags. I'm not allowed to disclose where.

Eventually I bought a house in Brooklyn. The trucks are pretty loud, but I've gotten used to them. And I like the idea that it is still a bit industrial. I don't like so much all the new condominiums that they are constructing. I sort of laugh inside when I realize that they are all screwed and they can't find people to live in their buildings.

One problem with the neighborhood is that all the hipsters are very selective of their coffee. They all clutter in this tiny, trendy coffee shop, and then the other shops go out of business. So I think on one hand, the hipster should be a little bit more tolerant of his coffee, because he's missing out on great places, and great mixture of culture. On the other hand, maybe some of the diners should buy an espresso machine.

NICK
DENTON

{ internet publisher

arrived: 2002 }

I once made a spreadsheet comparing San Francisco, London, Budapest, and New York. I assigned different weighted scores based on different criteria: old friends, business opportunities, Hungarians, Jews, nature (that one had a fairly low weight). I was living in San Francisco, but I've always liked the idea of that city more than the reality of it. So I would play with the spreadsheet, and when I didn't get the result I wanted, I adjusted the rankings. One factor that tipped things in New York's favor was that New York had hotter guys. (San Francisco is fine if you like blond hair and fleece.)

I finally decided to come here after 9/11. The foreign press was full of love letters to New York. Writers like Martin Amis were waking up and thinking, Oh my God, we almost lost it! I know it sounds sentimental, but no one would ever write a love letter to San Francisco. I drove across the country with Christian Bailey, who would later become famous for getting all that money from the Pentagon. He had arranged for a two-bedroom apartment in the SoHo Court building, a standard building for junior analysts at Goldman Sachs. It was a wonderful summer. I wasn't really working. We launched Gizmodo in August, and Gawker in December. Most days I would go to Cafe Gitane and sit outside eating waffles with fruit. I was early for every single lunch, because I was banking on San Francisco time—traffic, looking for parking—or London time— two train changes, a delay, time to wipe the sweat off your brow once you're out of the tube.

It was the year of the Hungarians. I was mainly

hanging out with friends I already knew, and feeling socially awkward after living in San Francisco. I remember going to a party with a bunch of Broadway and film gays, and the one-liner one-upmanship felt like a scene from *Will & Grace*, which at the time was my lame yardstick for what passed for New York salon conversation. My HTML skills had improved in San Francisco, but I'd lost my edge. I thought I was being really witty, but at one point on a ski trip to Tahoe, it became clear that everyone thought I was just an asshole.

KARA WALKER

{ artist
arrived: 2002 }

My daughter, Octavia, and I took the bus from Maine, where we had been living while my husband, Klaus, was teaching at the Maine College of Art. It was slow and arduous. There had been a blizzard. Getting off the Greyhound with a small child at the Port Authority, I felt like a woman of another era. We looked for a cabstand. A gypsy cab driver offered to get us a car. I wasn't sure if we wanted to do this, but when he showed us where the yellow taxis were waiting, it became clear that he was not a driver: he was a guy with no money who wanted a ride. Octavia was suspicious and scared. I didn't know how to say no. We all got in the cab, the man talking at me and thanking me. I spent the drive hoping Octavia wouldn't ask me, "Who is this man?"

I arrived in New York a sad wife and a successful artist and a weird mom all mixed up into one. I was thirty-two. I had an air mattress and, thanks to Columbia faculty housing, a two-bedroom apartment on Riverside and 116th Street with a partial water view. I wish I could say I loved New York when I got here, but I was afraid of it. I was exiting a protected phase in my life, and this was compounded by the insecurity of post-9/11 New York. I woke up on that first crisp January morning, gorgeous but freezing, and heard a horn going off across the Hudson that sounded like an air raid siren. I remember holding myself and saying, "Okay, is this it?" I waited a half hour and nothing happened. Then I thought, I'll get up and get through things.

That winter, Octavia spent two weeks in New York

with me, and then two weeks back in Maine with her father. There was a heat wave in March, and I remember taking Octavia back to Maine, where they still had icicles. The contrast was extreme.

In the spring, Octavia and I were at the playground, sitting on the low iron railing and waiting to use the swing. There was still tension in the air, the fear of any kind of terrorist attack. Suddenly, something happened. I couldn't tell what it was, but two police cars pulled up right outside the playground. I saw the police heading toward us. A man got panicky, grabbed his child, and ran. The screams of the children around me seemed to increase, so I threw Octavia to the ground and jumped on top of her. Then I looked around and saw . . . nothing had happened. The guy was getting a parking ticket.

All that year I was trying to force myself out of some kind of shell, and doing it in extremely awkward ways. I taught a couple of days a week. It was my first time teaching, and there were moments when I felt unqualified and angry with myself for making a move that was so hard. At Columbia, it felt like I was a little lamb who was befriended by all these really nice tigers and wolves. My colleagues were nice to me and gave me special favors, but I was always a little on edge, wondering what I was going to give back.

One day, I invited some colleagues and students over for drinks at my unfinished apartment. As drink parties go, it made me aware of the people I was not going to like, and also that I had a power I was not completely able to own up to. It was that feeling of being "on." I recognized that there were people in the room regarding me with envy and suspicion. One woman who used to be on the adjunct faculty would look at the way I broke open a bar of chocolate and say, "Do you always do it like that?"

In August, Klaus moved in. The sofa didn't fit in the elevator, so we had to throw it out. It was the first article of furniture I had ever bought, a cushy sofa that was great for falling asleep on. We could only salvage the pillows. That's a true New York moment: the eruption of frustration and capitulation when you have to saw the sofa in half.

It was still summer, and we were trying to understand the new family dynamic. New York was beautiful: the parks were in full swing, the little fountains were on in all the playgrounds. One of the unspoken tensions in the household was that this living in New

York thing was my project, so I had to make it work. We did everything the city had to offer: museums, street fairs, SummerStage. Or I was going to my studio and trying to fashion art, or at least seem like I was being the responsible breadwinner, which I resented.

The color of my life changed as I tried to undo my isolation, but it wasn't until the following fall that I would start to own my independence, feel more solid as an artist and a mother, and recognize that the most unstable portion of my life was my marriage. New York—the whole ambience of the city, its potential— was, in Klaus's eyes, a competition for affection. And he wouldn't join the party. But by then, I would be able to move in the circles that I wanted to move in, with or without him.

ASHLEY DUPRÉ

{ former escort }

arrived: 2004

New York was always my end goal, eyes on the prize. I was living in New Jersey with my grandfather, and commuting into the city to work doubles: eleven to five waiting tables at the Hotel Gansevoort during the day, then bottle-hosting at a club called Pangaea from ten until five in the morning. I got to be friends with a doorman there who would let me crash at his place on Forty-sixth Street—right there in Times Square, near Little Brazil Street. But it was rough. I was sleeping whenever I could, barely. I hit a low point when I wrecked my Jetta going over the bridge back to Jersey. I was sober, but I had passed out at the wheel, exhausted. That was when I knew something needed to change.

One day I was at that guy's place on Forty-sixth, and the landlord told me there's an opening in 3A. My eyes just lit up, like in cartoons. I remember going to see the $2,100 one-bedroom, with its white walls and big windows, and my brain started working immediately on how to get this. A few days later, I shared a cab with an aspiring model—a total stranger—and within fifteen minutes we had decided to live together in this apartment. It was one of those things that happen like the city is working for you.

It always feels like that when you're young. I was eighteen, and it was the party scene: Marquee, Suede, Butter, and we'd always end up at Bungalow 8—that was our spot to regroup. Everything felt amazing. I remember thinking, Seriously, I'm getting paid for bottle hosting? I was this naive little girl, really. Because, honestly? You can all hang out and be buddy-buddy and whatever, but at the end of the day you've got to make it work for yourself. When that model left the apartment, reality sank in, and I was always worrying about paying rent. My girlfriends and I could go out on a date any night of the week and get a free meal—there was always that option. But most of the time I was sitting at home eating peanut butter and apples. What else was I going to do, eat the roaches? Grab a mouse and fry it up?

I'd go to the stores on that stretch of Fifth—Chanel, YSL, Cartier, Gucci, Louis Vuitton—and I'd look and touch, but I wouldn't try anything on. Can you imagine how depressing? To try them on in the mirror and then have to put them back? I never did that unless I could afford it. I protected myself like that.

It's not like I was bedazzled by New York, but I do remember one time when I was eating at DB, I looked up to see Steven Spielberg, his wife, and Michelle Pfeiffer. I had grown up on *Grease 2*. Michelle Pfeiffer's life was something I had admired and always wanted for myself. She was so gorgeous. I just stared.

ZOE
KAZAN

{ actress
arrived: 2005 }

I fell in love with New York that year because I wasn't planning on staying. I had moved here because I wanted to be close to my boyfriend. I took a few classes at The Actors Center, and was planning to enroll in the Yale School of Drama the following year.

I had arranged my financial aid and shipped all

my stuff back to my parents' house in Los Angeles. But then I went back to visit them and had a panic attack. I had an agent at that point, and I couldn't figure out why I was going to grad school. I felt like I was going to die if I moved to New Haven, and I was so homesick for New York that I watched the American Express advertisement with De Niro talking about TriBeCa and I started to cry. I thought, I have to go home! I called the head of the drama school and told him I wouldn't be attending. And then I e-mailed all my friends: "I need an apartment."

I stayed in a lot of places that first year, including a loft in TriBeCa I shared with Brazilians who would play music until five in the morning. But I eventually settled into my first real apartment in the East Village. It was heaven, and it felt like the beginning of my adult life. So I bought a bed, and the day I moved in I got my first real acting job: the role of Sandy in *The Prime of Miss Jean Brodie*. I was painting the wall of my room when I got the call.

It was such a hard year! I was trying to figure out how to be an adult. I made so many mistakes, and though I think I needed help I didn't know how to ask for it. There was never a part of me that thought I wouldn't get work as an actor. And I don't think that comes from talent; I'm just one of the most hardworking people I know. I'd always been an "A" student and done six plays a year. But then I got to New York and I didn't know how to do it right. I didn't know how to feed or dress myself. I'd see girls my age on the street with impeccable boots with fur at the top, and the fur wasn't matted! How did they get there? I had to work hard to keep clean underwear in the house. I didn't know that when things go wrong you are supposed to tell the super.

I broke up with my boyfriend and spent the following months getting to know the men of New York. I slept with a lot of people. I'd never done something like that before, and I've never done it again, but it was definitely fun and it expanded my horizons. I wore a lot of eye makeup that year. I looked tough; it was like armor. It was definitely the most un-girly I've ever dressed. I didn't wear a bra.

I met a lot of friends too. We'd go ice-skating in Bryant Park in the middle of the day, or to clubs that only this person knows about or this person can get you in. The funny part was that at the same time I was living this incredibly ascetic life—not spending much, taking money from my parents and feeling bad about that. I ate bagels three times a day, and a lot of yogurt. I started drinking coffee, because it's cheap at the bodega and it made me feel like a New Yorker to be walking around with a cup of coffee.

I felt so connected to my father that year, thinking about how he grew up in New York. And my grandfather and his parents came to America through Ellis Island, and even now when I see the Statue of Liberty while taking the Q train over the river, it's really moving. New York is like being in a good relationship, where you remember the first days—but it can also feel sometimes like the first days again.

In retrospect, I cringe at everything I did and wore that year. I wish I hadn't been so friendly with so many people, because I'm not good at making casual friends and ended up letting people down. But at the time, I thought I was having the best year of my life. Just walking around New York with my iPod was an adventure. I remember my first audition, for a two-page scene on a *Law & Order* episode. I was walking to Chelsea Piers because I didn't yet know how to take the bus, and suddenly I realized, Oh, it's never going to be this good again. If I get the job, I'm always going to want to get the job again. But for right now, I'm just happy to have the audition. And I have to remember this feeling.

AGYNESS DEYN

{ model
arrived: 2006 }

The only people I knew when I arrived were the band the Five O'Clock Heroes. They took me under their wing and got me a room with one of their mates. It was an office on West Tenth Street. I don't know what they did there; I would come in and they were all at computers, on the phone. I just would run in and sleep.

When I first got here, I would wake up, grab my

iPod, and just walk around. Then I got a bike, and I would ride everywhere—uptown, downtown, exploring. I loved how fresh New York was. I felt like I was the star of my own Woody Allen film. At nights I'd go out on my own to bars like Black and White, and parties like Misshapes. It was nerve-racking. But usually I'd get a drink, have a walk around, talk to someone at the bar, and then meet some of that person's friends and maybe go on to a loft party in Williamsburg.

One day, I came across Trash and Vaudeville and tried on some jeans. I was gutted that I had just missed CBGB down the street, where I had read that the Ramones and Blondie had played. The guy at the checkout counter, Jimmy, looked like Iggy Pop, all rock and roll in his leather pants and long scraggly blond hair. He looked at me and went, "No, no, no," and got me the smallest-size jeans in the store. "The tighter the better, darling." After that, I would go into Trash and Vaudeville whenever I was at a loose end or feeling lonely. I'd sit there and chat with Jimmy, and he'd tell me old stories of New York.

JAMES FRANCO

{ actor and student }

arrived: 2008

I moved at the end of August. I had just come from summer school in Paris and promoting *Pineapple Express* in Europe, so I was only able to get here the day before orientation. I found a West Village apartment that I was told the B-52s used to own. It's close enough to NYU, where I'm enrolled in film school at Tisch, and also the subway to Columbia, where I'm in the creative writing program.

I'd never really taken the subway before. I love it! The one thing is, I used to listen to a lot of audio books in my car in L.A., and now I don't have that. It's almost a shame. Now I'll go on long walks and listen to them.

I go to the Columbia library all the time. Everybody used to come up to me in the library. Then I realized I was in the one room people are free to talk in. Now I go to the quiet room.

NATE
SILVER

{ political analyst
arrived: 2009 }

I've been here six months and change, I guess. I'd
been living in Chicago since 1996, when I started at
the University of Chicago. Back then Barack Obama
was my state senator, so I'd known about him long
before the speech at the 2004 convention. When he
ran for president it was like having one of your neighbors run. That was one of the reasons I got heavily

involved in politics. I'd mostly been writing about baseball, but you start thinking, Hey do I want to be writing about baseball for my whole life? So I started writing as a diarist on Daily Kos and migrated off to start my own website, FiveThirtyEight.com. So much political coverage is ideologically driven; I wanted to gather the evidence, to be scientific about it. Mostly I wanted to decode the polls for people. By the time we got to Labor Day 2008, we had twenty-five to thirty polls coming out. How do you synthesize them to just one number: who's going to win?

Those last few months in Chicago got so busy with the success of FiveThirtyEight, I barely even remember them. I was sleeping four or five hours a day, bouncing back and forth between writing on the website, going to the political conventions, and flying to New York every three weeks to do a media hit or take a meeting or to visit friends. If you're in the political world overlapping with media and tech worlds, New York is the nexus of people and ideas. At one point I noticed I had more New York cell phone numbers in my Black-Berry than Chicago numbers.

In Chicago you might look for an apartment two months in advance; in New York it's more like the week before. I didn't know where I wanted to live. I almost moved to the West Village but at the grocery across the street it was $15 for a six-pack of beer. I finally found a place in Brooklyn Heights through a broker. I had assumed I'd be paying twice as much as in Chicago, which was $1,250—so double that, and that was my budget. Then I kept going up from there.

The promise that attracted me to move is the idea that you can come to New York and be surrounded by the people who are the best at what they do in many different fields. On that front, I think it delivers. Working your way around the city you really do run into a disproportionate number of really interesting people. That's almost what you pay your taxes for, even if you think it's a little crazy to pay that much to live here. People in New York are a lot busier than those in Chicago, more direct and more social. Chicago isn't cliquish exactly but a little more inwardly focused, a bit more comfy, and you're probably more satisfied with your station in life. People in Chicago get into their thirties and have a family and stay in, whereas in New York you have people of all ages going out. You'll see a fifty- or sixty-year-old couple out on a date.

There are things I miss, of course. There's not really that much good Mexican food in New York; your rent check is two to three times more than you had to pay before; the airports are really awful and the baseball stadiums are far away. In Chicago, I could catch a cab and be at Wrigley Field in ten minutes. And Wrigley still caters to the common fan—unintentionally, because it's older. They haven't yet innovated ways to maximize profit, like having luxury boxes. Madison Square Garden is like that a bit, too—you don't have a whole tier of luxury suites that move the proletariat up thirty feet and make their view worse. The first time I went to Yankee Stadium, a guy ordered a hot dog and Merlot. Then he sent the Merlot back. You're just not allowed to order a glass of Merlot at a baseball game! And if you do, you're sure as hell not allowed to send it back.

Chicago is also a bit more compact—you can go from A to B in ten or fifteen minutes, it seems. My first week in New York, I was running late for a panel at Columbia and I was in Park Slope; I was like, Oh, I'll just take a cab. Big mistake time-wise and financially. You wind up spending a lot of money here without even meaning to.

But I look at it from an economist's point of view:

you pay a premium to live here for access to food and culture. And New York tends to attract people who want to participate in the life of the city, which I think by and large are people who are outgoing and interested, networking and working hard but having fun. Here you're always trying to reach for something— maybe you don't even know what, exactly.

JENNY JOSLIN

{ aspiring actress

arrived: 2009 }

The *New York Times* took my picture the first day I was here. A feature on Koreatown; it was incredibly unflattering and I was eating yogurt. But I knew it was some sort of omen, a sign that I belonged. I had just graduated from Texas State University and had come to New York to perform in an acting showcase. About ten people showed up.

I was half certain I would be employed with an acting job within the week, and half scared out of my mind. My first three days, I ate CarrotTop Chicken Caesar salads on my bed while searching the trade papers for auditions and Craigslist for a server job. My roommate, Curt, hadn't furnished the apartment, so we shopped the streets for furniture, yelling "Curb alert!" and checking for bedbugs. (If it didn't have a red "X", it was fine.)

After about a week, I had my first New York breakdown at an interview for a server position in the Financial District. (They gave me a timed math test; I couldn't remember any equations and began to sob.) I rode the A train to open calls for original plays, arriving hours ahead of time because I was terrified of being late. Listening to the other actors talk made me feel like a foreigner. In fact, the *auditioning* part of auditions became much less horrifying than this new social anxiety I had developed. Auditions were proving fruitless. I spent a few days in bed wondering who was this cowardly sloth-girl whose hands would start shaking at an audition and who couldn't afford a Wendy's cheeseburger? Curt finally took me to a nearby bar and we drank a pitcher of Sangria.

I asked if they were hiring. That's the day I became a bartender.

Things have changed. I've started to embrace the heightened insanity that is New York reality, and to welcome daily bits of crazed wisdom. When an older gentleman in driving gloves pulled over his Lexus on Prince Street to tell me I looked like Rita Hayworth, I agreed to a glass of wine across the street. He told me stories about the city, and about restaurants I can't afford to eat in. One night bar-hopping in the West Village, Curt and I met a cute boy in the street who invited us to Alan Cumming's CD release party at The Box. I found myself standing next to Julie Taymor, practicing nonchalance and hoping the safety-pinned rip in my thrift store dress wasn't showing. I left my phone in a cab that night only to have it deposited at the desk of a hotel. The next morning I walked through Times Square to retrieve it and marveled at my luck.

Acknowledgments

This book originated as a cover feature in the April 20, 2009, issue of *New York* magazine, and as such it relied on the talents of a small army of editors, writers, reporters, photography editors, and designers.

All of the pieces that first ran in the magazine—and many of the ones that were gathered since—began as interviews with a reporter, and were edited and condensed by the magazine. We are grateful to all of the reporters who contributed to this project, including: Molly Bennet, Rebecca Bengal, Fiona Byrne, Katie Charles, Brian Thomas Gallagher, Darrell Hartman, Helin Jung, Ben Leventhal, Nina Mandell, Rebecca Milzoff, Emma Pearse, Meg Prossnitz, Diana Scholl, Joshua David Stein, and Ross Kenneth Urken. Jada Yuan and Jared Hohlt deserve particular thanks for their help in gathering and editing the material.

The expansion of this feature into a book would not have been possible without Matt Weiland, who proposed a collaboration with Ecco/HarperCollins hours after the issue hit the newsstands. Matt knew exactly what this book could be and proved masterful at helping us realize it. This is his book as much as it is ours. We are grateful to everyone else at Ecco, too, for their warm enthusiasm and strong support for the book, especially Daniel Halpern, Rachel Bressler, Ginny Smith, and Michael McKenzie.

The following people also deserve special thanks: David McCormick of McCormick & Williams, for his care and calm representing the magazine as our agent, as well as Ann Clarke, Kit Taylor, and Lauren Starke at *New York* for helping, in different ways, to shepherd the project through to completion. Serena Torrey was indispensable, especially in the book's crucial early stages. Richard Morgan and Tim Murphy, two gifted journalists who conducted the vast majority of the additional interviews, played a critical role in shaping the book's content. Ira Boudway and Eric Benson fact-checked and provided research assistance. Michael Idov helped craft the book's preface. And finally, Chris Dixon; Ecco's art director, Allison Saltzman; and the illustrator Klas Fahlén all had their hands in designing the lovely cover of this volume.

Most profoundly, we would like to thank the fifty-six individuals who shared with us their first memories of New York. They spoke with candor and eloquence (and awesome powers of recollection), and helped us see our city with fresh eyes, again and again.

About *New York* Magazine

Since 1968, *New York* magazine has aimed to reflect back at its readers the energy and excitement of the city itself. With assertive reporting, stylish writing, and elegant photography and design, the magazine chronicles the people and events that are forever reshaping New York.

In addition to its weekly magazine, the *New York* family includes nymag.com, an up-to-the-minute news and information website about New York and the New York worldview; Vulture.com, a site for entertainment news and analysis; the fashion site The Cut; and Grub Street, a national network of food blogs.

About the Editors

DAVID HASKELL is Features Editor at *New York* magazine.

ADAM MOSS is the Editor-in-Chief at *New York* magazine.